drape drape

Hisako Sato

Laurence King Publishing

Hisako Sato

Hisako Sato graduated from the Fashion Design program at Bunka Fashion College, Japan, in 1986, leaving to work for a major apparel manufacturer. In 1990, she was appointed head of garment design at Muji, before becoming an independent designer in 1993. In 1994, Hisako Sato made her debut at Tokyo Collection (now Japan Fashion Week) with the Beige shop brand. She is currently producing new collections as a designer for the Raw+ brand: www.rawtus.com

LAURENCE KING

Published in 2012 by
Laurence King Publishing Ltd
361–373 City Road
London EC1V 1LR
United Kingdom
Tel: + 44 20 7841 6900
Fax: + 44 20 7841 6910
e-mail: enquiries@laurenceking.com
www.laurenceking.com

Reprinted 2012, 2013, 2014, 2015

Drape Drape by Hisako Sato
Copyright © Hisako Sato 2009
Original Japanese edition published by EDUCATIONAL FOUNDATION BUNKA GAKUEN, BUNKA PUBLISHING BUREAU.

This English edition is published by arrangement with EDUCATIONAL FOUNDATION BUNKA GAKUEN, BUNKA PUBLISHING BUREAU, Tokyo, in care of Tuttle-Mori Agency, Inc., Tokyo.

A catalogue record for this book is available from the British Library.

ISBN: 978-1-85669-841-2

Typeface: Sabon and Syntax
Printed in China

Contents

I love to design, and have worked on all kinds of clothing over many years as a designer.

More recently, as part of the fun of the design experience, I've been turning my hand to production.

Of the garments I've produced in the last five or six years, a number featuring draping techniques have made their way onto the racks. I've continued to incorporate these effects into my own designs, greatly increasing the variety of techniques at my disposal.

The term "drape" has acquired the connotation of being a rather feminine skill, but this is not the case.

Unlike designs where a number of cutting lines are added to a single piece of fabric, draped designs emerge from the way the slack in the different materials brings out the character of the textile, and from the detail in the lines sketched out by the grain of the fabric.

Delicate drapes made from thin, soft fabrics, falling drapes produced by stretch materials, loose drapes created by the varying slackness of the fabrics, gather drapes, and tuck drapes (the names of which should be self-explanatory) have all come together to produce this book, which I have called *Drape Drape*.

The clothes I present in *Drape Drape* range from simple, relaxed garments to evening dresses, and are designed for the pleasure of working with a variety of draping effects.

no.1 loose drape top + tuck drape pants
see pages 15, 18 for instructions

How to make the garments

About the sizes used and the full-scale patterns included with this book

You will find full-scale patterns for all of the pieces featured in *Drape Drape* at the back of this book. However, while some of the designs are for a one-size garment, others can be made in either two sizes (S/M and M/L), or four sizes (S, M, L, and XL).

Please consult the size chart when choosing the pattern size.

The full-scale patterns all include seam allowances. Take care when copying the patterns, because the shapes of the seam allowances and positions of the notches are very important when folding tucks and creating other effects.

The techniques we will be using to create the garments featured in *Drape Drape* are: slack (photograph 1), tuck (photograph 2), gather (photograph 3), and finally drape drape (photograph 4), which brings all of these techniques together.

The key to each of them is the beauty of movement inherent in the fabric. Various materials are used in this book: cotton, wool, tricot, and silk. The best way to achieve the garments in the way they are shown in *Drape Drape* is to use an identical material, but for many of them you may not be able to get hold of exactly the same fabric. The flow and volume of the drape will change somewhat with the material, which should present you with some enjoyable challenges!

	Size chart (cm)				
	Size	S	M	L	XL
	Height	153	158	163	168
Body	Bust	78	82	86	90
measurements	Waist	58	62	66	70
	Hips	84	88	92	96

1

2

3

4

Materials

Knitted fabrics made from standard cotton and wool are not difficult to handle. However, knitted fabrics such as doubleknit (double rib) (photograph 1) and jersey (plain knit) (photograph 2) that stretch even when made from cotton, wool, or silk, as well as tricots and other fabrics where the yarn itself is stretchy, demand different needles, thread, and methods of sewing. I have covered ways to deal with stretch materials as well as woven fabrics, and on page 11 you will find a detailed description of the basic method for sewing stretch materials.

Preparation

1 Grain mending

Cotton and wool may shrink when exposed to steam or moisture from a steam iron, and the fabric itself may warp, so it makes sense to mend the grain before cutting.

With woven fabrics (photograph 3), first remove the weft and cut straight along the raw edge. With lace fabrics that have no weft to remove (photograph 4), cut using the pattern of the material as a guide. In the case of knitted fabrics such as doubleknit (double rib) (photograph 1) and jersey (plain knit) (photograph 2), however, do not remove the thread, whether the fabric is made from cotton, wool, or silk. Cut gently straight along the cross-stitch instead.

Cotton should then be soaked for two to three hours and dried in a shaded place, without being wrung out. Iron while damp. If the raw edges do not meet when the fabric is folded in two to bring the selvages together, it means that the material has warped. Pull the material in the direction of the bias (the opposite direction to the warp) to adjust the grain, then iron.

With wool, run a steam iron over the entire fabric, adjusting the grain so that the horizontal and vertical stitches become perpendicular.

With silk, simply run a dry iron over the entire fabric to adjust the grain.

Doubleknit (double rib)—In lock-knits, the same stitch is visible on both the upside and the wrong side (reverse), and the raw edges lie flat.

Jersey (plain knit)—In flat-knits, the appearance of the stitch is different on the upside and the wrong side (reverse). Raw edges are easily rolled to the upside.

1

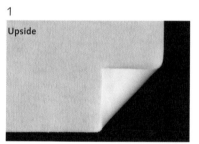
Upside

2

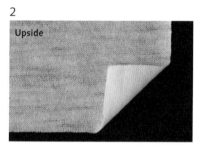
Upside

3

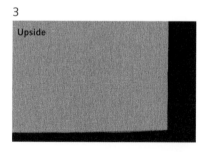
Upside

4

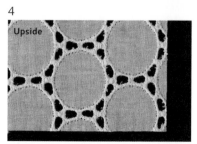
Upside

2 Cutting and marking

On symmetrical designs, fold the fabric in two on the outside, place the pattern (including the seam allowances) over it, and weigh it down. Indicate the cutting line with chalk (photograph 1). Gently remove the pattern without moving the two layers of fabric, and resecure the edge of the cutting line with marking pins. Cut with scissors following the marked cutting line. If the cloth slips noticeably as a result of being forced by the blades when using scissors to cut stretch materials, tricot, and other such fabrics in two layers, make a mark to the left and right of the cutting line on each layer to give improved cutting accuracy. Snip notches (of around 5 mm) into the markings, tacking with tacking thread if you have a number of tucks that are difficult to make out using just notches. During this process, you can change the color of the tacking thread on the mountain and valley folds to ensure that the tuck is folded in the correct direction (see pattern no.16, figures A and B).

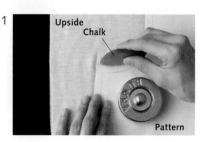
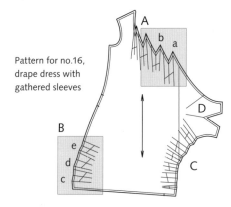

Pattern for no.16, drape dress with gathered sleeves

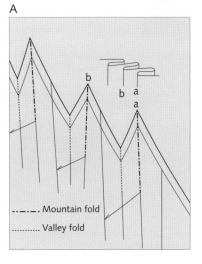

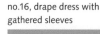

no.16, drape dress with gathered sleeves

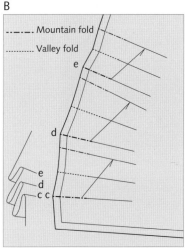
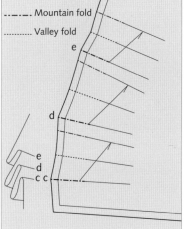

..—.—.. Mountain fold

.... Valley fold

3 Interlining

Add fusible interlining to the facing and other areas that you want to secure firmly. To create fusible interlining, align the fusible side with the reverse of the fabric and press lightly with a dry iron to secure temporarily in place. To ensure that the adhesive does not seep onto the iron from the fabric backing of the interlining, cover with kraft or tracing paper, or a damp cloth, and iron firmly. Fabric with fusible interlining can easily kink while cooling, so take care not to move it. When applying woven fusible stay tape, place 2 to 3mm over the stitching line on straight seam lines such as shoulder lines in order to prevent stretching. If you are applying tape to curved areas such as the armholes, first gently apply it to the outer edge of the seam line, where the measurement is longer, and then iron the fusible stay tape flat (photograph 3). In the case of stretch materials, apply knitted fusible stretch tape (photograph 4) if you want to fit the tape to the stretchiness of the material without actually stretching it. The area with the fusible stay tape will be surprisingly firm. I have not applied tape to the neckline and armhole areas which will be hemmed, but if they do end up stretching anyway, cut the tape finely so that it fits inside the width of the hem when you apply it.

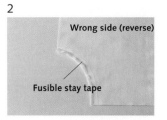

Wrong side (reverse)

Fusible stay tape

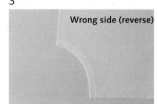

Wrong side (reverse)

Folding a tuck

See no.16 drape dress with gathered sleeves, area A

In photograph 1, I have added precise cutting marks to
a piece of fabric that I am folding, using the pattern to
check the direction of the tucks. Align the raw edges of
the seam allowance carefully when making these folds
(photographs 2 and 3). Insert marking pins and tack
immediately along the seam allowance (photograph 4),
then fold area B in the same way (photographs 5 to 7).
Continue by folding C and D, paying careful attention
to the variations in the direction of the tucks in each
case (photographs 8 and 9).

5

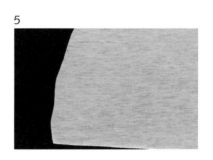

6

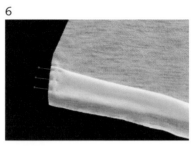

7

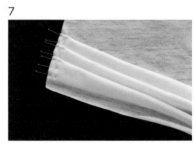

1

Upside

2

3

4

Tacking

8

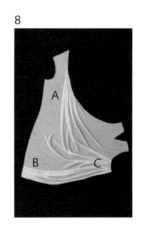

A

B   C

9

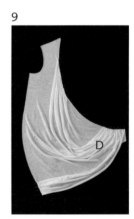

D

Gathering in

Sew large gathered stitches along the seam-allowance
side of the finishing line, and pull on either the needle
thread or the bobbin thread to gather the fabric.
Placing the fabric on an ironing mat and fixing the
other end of the thread with a marking pin will make it
easier to gather (photograph 10). Arrange the folds in
the gather, running an iron over the seam allowance to
flatten it down as you work (photograph 11).

10

Upside

11

Basic sewing method for stretch materials

Needle and thread

Make sure you have a needle and thread that are designed specifically for use on stretch materials, as this will allow you to sew most stretch materials more easily. The sewing needle should be a ball-point needle specially designed for knitted fabrics, which is long from eye to tip (photograph 1). It will exert only a light pressure on the material, making it easy to sew and preventing the foundation yarn from breaking. For the sewing thread, use Resilon or Leona 66, which are specially designed for knitted textiles and, being made from nylon, will stretch ever so slightly to fit with the movements of the fabric (photograph 2). Thread designed for non-knit fabrics will fail to stretch with the material and result in broken yarn, so be sure to use thread that is intended for use with knit fabric.

1

2

Standard, zigzag, and overlock-stitch sewing machines

Although the designs can be sewn with just a standard straight-line or zigzag sewing machine, soft, thin knit fabrics may contract when you run a zigzag machine on them (photograph 3), so always do a test run before you begin. In situations like this, finishing raw edges by running a zigzag machine on a single layer of fabric is probably best avoided. To finish raw edges, I recommend an overlock-stitch machine (photographs 4 and 5), which will allow you to sew neatly and rapidly. A coverstitch machine or specialist interlock sewing machine (photograph 6) that allows you to over-edge and lap-seam the raw edges in one go, such as when taking the hem up on a T-shirt, will also be useful.

This section describes the basic sewing method for each type of sewing machine, so that you can choose the one that suits the machine you have available to you.

3

4

5

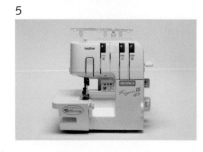

6

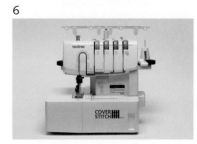

Basic sewing

When you use a sewing machine on stretch materials or knitted fabrics, finishing the raw edges on a single layer of fabric can be enough to cause a degree of stretching. Instead, first machine-sew the seam line on two layers of overlapped fabric and then finish with either of the methods described below.

Finishing seam lines—opening the seam

Stay stitching (photographs 1 to 3)

Align the fabric wrong side (reverse) out and stitch along the seam line. Open the seam allowance from the seam line and add stay stitches 3 mm from the raw edge.

With thin and soft knitted fabrics, the start of the seam may get dragged into the needle location so that the stitches become packed together. If you are using this kind of fabric, lay a piece of kraft or tracing paper under the fabric and stitch them together (photograph 4). When you have finished stitching, tear the paper off gently so that it does not pull the thread from the stitches.

Triple overlocked stitches (photographs 5 to 7)

Align the fabric wrong side (reverse) out and stitch along the seam line. Open the seam allowance from the seam line and overlock-stitch the raw edge.

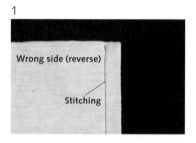

1

Wrong side (reverse)

Stitching

2

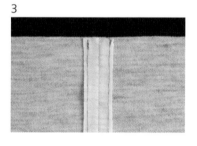

3

5

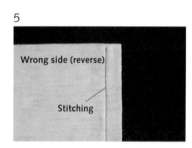

Wrong side (reverse)

Stitching

6

4

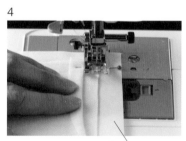

Kraft or tracing paper

7

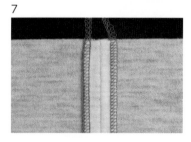

Finishing the seam allowance—flat felling

Stay stitching (photographs 1 to 3)

Align the fabric wrong side (reverse) out and stitch along the seam line. Add stay stitches 3 mm from the raw edge. Open the fabric out, turn the seam allowance to one side of the seam line, and press with an iron.

1

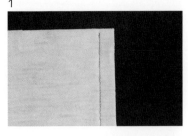

2

3

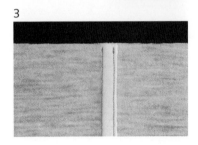

Triple overlocked stitches (photographs 4 to 6)

Align the fabric wrong side (reverse) out and stitch along the seam line. Overlock-stitch the seam allowance on both layers together. Open the fabric out, turn the seam allowance to one side of the seam line, and press with an iron.

4

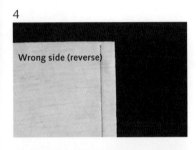

Wrong side (reverse)

5

6

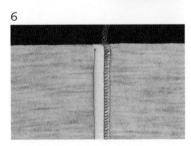

Zigzag stitching (photographs 7 to 9)

Align the fabric wrong side (reverse) out and stitch along the seam line. Zigzag-stitch the seam allowance on both layers together. Open the fabric out, turn the seam allowance to one side of the seam line, and press with an iron.

7

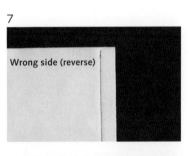

Wrong side (reverse)

8

9

Four-thread (quadruple) overlocked stitches (photographs 10 to 11)

Four-thread (quadruple) overlocked stitching also doubles as a plain seam, so align the fabric wrong side (reverse) out and overlock-stitch the seam line. Open the fabric out, turn the seam allowance to one side of the seam line, and press with an iron.

10

Wrong side (reverse)

11

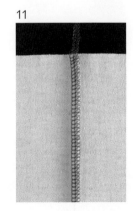

Taking the hem up—doubling up

Stay stitching (photographs 1 to 2)
Use an iron to double up the hem from the finishing line. Stitch the seam allowance to hold it in place.

Triple overlocked stitches (photographs 3 to 5)
Overlock-stitch the raw edge of the seam allowance. Use an iron to double up the hem from the finishing line. Stitch along the overlock-stitched seam to hold it in place.

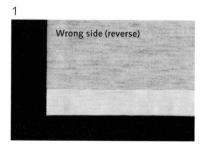

Four-thread (quadruple) overlocked stitches (photographs 6 to 7)

Stitching that allows you to hold folded-up fabric in place with a double-width chain stitch that resembles an overlock-stitched seam. If you stitch in such a way that the fabric goes onto the raw edge of the seam allowance, it is possible to finish and lap-seam the edges in one go, although you will not be able to trim the fabric while you stitch as with standard overlocked stitching.

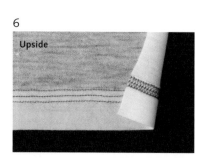

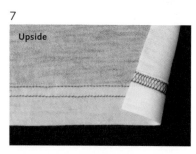

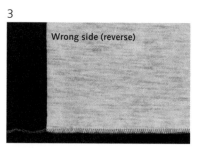

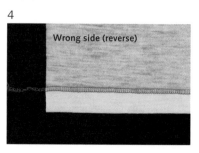

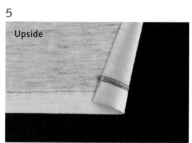

no.1 loose drape top

◆ **Required patterns (side A):**

front, back, hemming fabric.

◆ **Sewing instructions**

1 Sew up the shoulders and flat-fell the seam allowance to the back.
2 Finish the edges of the facing on the neckline with a narrow rolled hem.
3 Fold the neckline facing to the finishing line.
4 Hem the armholes (see figure 4).
5 Sew up the sides and flat-fell the seam allowance to the back.
6 Fold up the hem, and stitch.

◆ **Widths and lengths used**

Materials: silk and wool jersey (plain knit)
= W 140 cm
(S, M) 80 cm
(L, XL) 90 cm

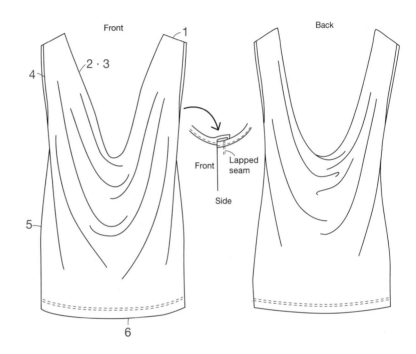

Front

Back

Lapped seam

Front

Side

4 Armhole hemming

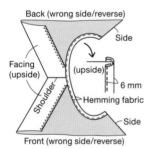

Back (wrong side/reverse)

Side

Facing (upside)

(upside)

6 mm

Hemming fabric

Shoulder

Side

Front (wrong side/reverse)

See p. 71 for instructions on hemming

Cutting layout

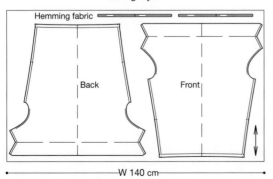

Hemming fabric

Back

Front

W 140 cm

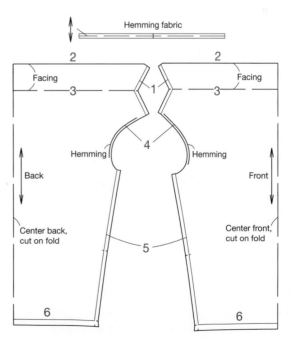

Hemming fabric

Facing

Facing

Back

Front

Hemming

Hemming

Center back, cut on fold

Center front, cut on fold

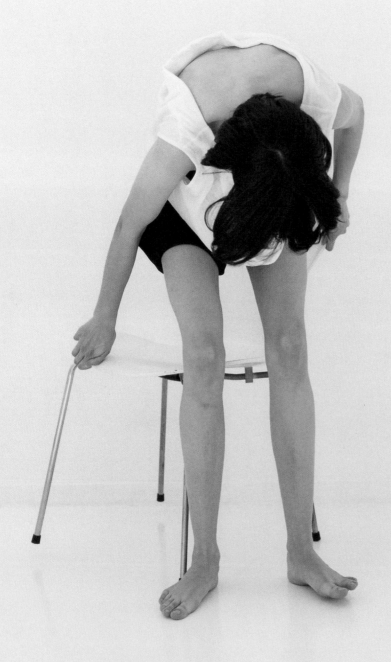

no.1 loose drape top + tuck drape pants
see pages 15, 18 for instructions

no.1 tuck drape pants

◆ **Required patterns (side A):**

front, back, waistband, cuffs.

◆ **Sewing instructions**

1 Sew up the center front and back seams (rises).
2 Fold the waist tucks at the front and back and tack in place (see figure 2).
3 Sew the sides together.
4 Sew the inseams together so they are adjoining.
5 Sew the sides of the waistband and the inseam of the cuffs together to form a loop. Leave an opening through which you will pass the elastic tape, unsewn at this stage (see figure 5).
6 Attach the waistband (see figure 6).
7 Attach the cuffs.
8 Pass the elastic tape through the waistband and cuffs.

◆ **Widths and lengths used**

Material: polyester doubleknit
   (double rib)
= W 150 cm
(S, M) 2 m
(L, XL) 2 m 20 cm
3 cm-wide elastic tape, to fit

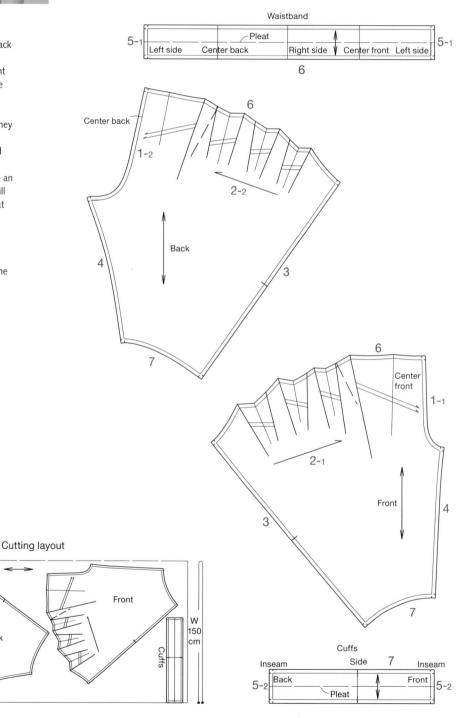

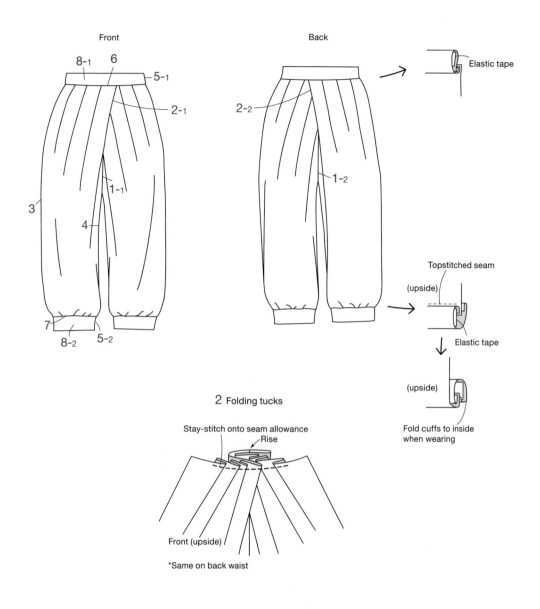

Front

8-1   6
        —5-1
        —2-1

1-1
3
4

7
8-2   5-2

Back

Elastic tape

2-2
1-2

Topstitched seam

(upside)

Elastic tape

(upside)

Fold cuffs to inside when wearing

2 Folding tucks

Stay-stitch onto seam allowance
Rise

Front (upside)

*Same on back waist

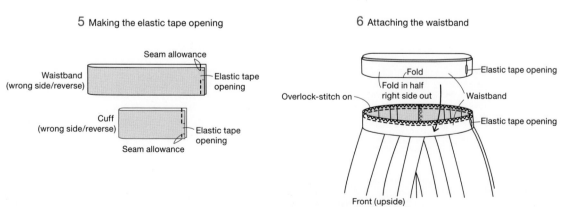

5 Making the elastic tape opening

Seam allowance

Waistband
(wrong side/reverse)
Elastic tape
opening

Cuff
(wrong side/reverse)
Elastic tape
opening

Seam allowance

6 Attaching the waistband

Fold
Elastic tape opening

Fold in half
right side out

Overlock-stitch on
Waistband

Elastic tape opening

Front (upside)

no.2 gather drape cape jacket + gather drape pants
see pages 22, 24 for instructions

no.3 drop-waist gather drape dress
see page 26 for instructions

no.2 gather drape cape jacket

◆ **Required patterns (side A):**

front, front side, back, back panel, back hem, back side, side panel, cape, hemming fabric.

◆ **Sewing instructions**

1 Sew each of the following parts to begin with: the center backs of the upside of the back fabric, the lining of the back fabric, the upside of the back hem, and the wrong side (reverse) of the back hem.

2 Sew the upside and lining of the back panel, the bodice back, and the back hem fabric.

3 Sew each of the shoulders on the upside and lining of the bodice.

4 Align the upside and lining of the bodice from step 3, wrong side (reverse) out, and edge-stitch (lap-seam) the front hem, neckline, and back hem.

5 Sew up the sides of the bodice front and back, blindstitch the inside of the hem, and hem the armholes (see figure 5).

6 Finish the top and bottom of the side panel with a threefold edge-stitched seam and gather at both sides.

7 Finish the outer perimeter of the cape with a threefold edge-stitched seam and gather at the attachment points.

8 Attach the bodice side, side panel, and cape together to the bodice front and back from step 4 (see figure 8).

9 Make the buttonholes and attach the buttons.

◆ **Widths and lengths used**

Material: serge
= W 140 cm x L 70 cm
Material: wool gauze
= W 140 cm
(S) 1 m
(M) 1 m 10 cm
(L) 1 m 20 cm
(XL) 1 m 30 cm
Other fabric: matte jersey
    (plain knit)
= W 140 cm x L 60 cm
12 mm-diameter buttons x 6

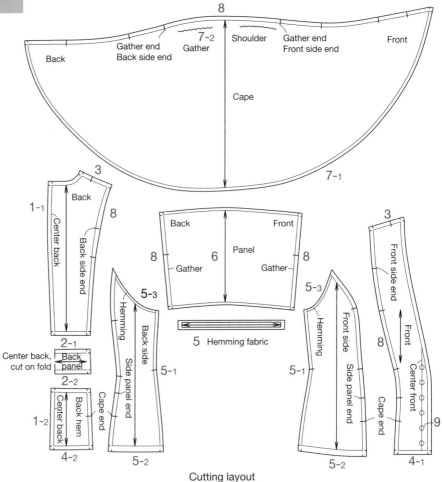

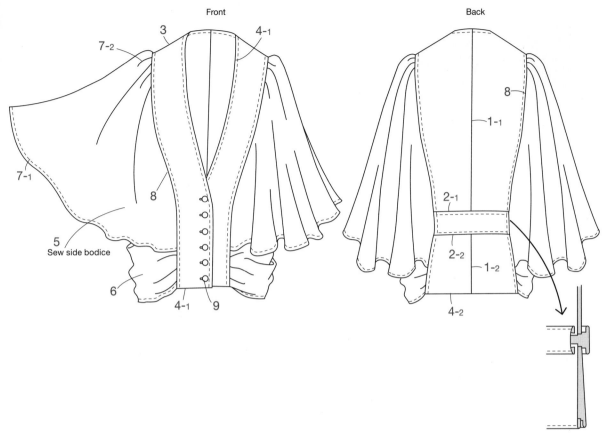

Front

7-2
3
4-1
7-1
8
5
Sew side bodice
6
4-1
9

Back

8
1-1
2-1
2-2
1-2
4-2

5 Sewing the side fabric

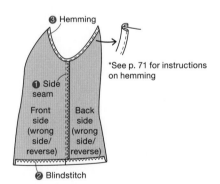

❸ Hemming

*See p. 71 for instructions on hemming

❶ Side seam

Front side (wrong side/ reverse)

Back side (wrong side/ reverse)

❷ Blindstitch

Other fabric

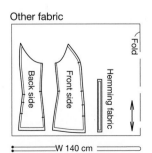

Fold

Back side

Front side

Hemming fabric

•— W 140 cm —•

8 Attaching the side bodice, side panel, and cape

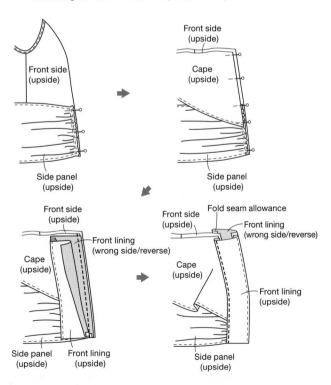

Front side (upside)

Side panel (upside)

Front side (upside)

Cape (upside)

Side panel (upside)

Front side (upside)

Cape (upside)

Front lining (wrong side/reverse)

Side panel (upside)

Front lining (upside)

Front side (upside)

Fold seam allowance

Front lining (wrong side/reverse)

Cape (upside)

Front lining (upside)

Side panel (upside)

no.2 gather drape pants

◆ **Required patterns (side A):**

front, back, front and back waistband fabric.

◆ **Sewing instructions**

1 Fold up the hem, and stitch.
2 Sew the front and back sides together.
3 Sew the front and back inseams together.
4 Stretch and attach elastic tape to the seam allowance, on the hem, at the sides, and inseams (see figure 4).
5 Sew up the waistband fabric on either side to form a loop.
6 Gather in the waist of the pants (see figure 6).
7 Stretch the waistband fabric and sew it onto the waist of the pants.

◆ **Widths and lengths used**

Material: cotton jersey (plain knit)
= W 135 cm
(S, M) 2 m 10 cm
(L, XL) 2 m 30 cm
5 mm-wide elastic tape, to fit

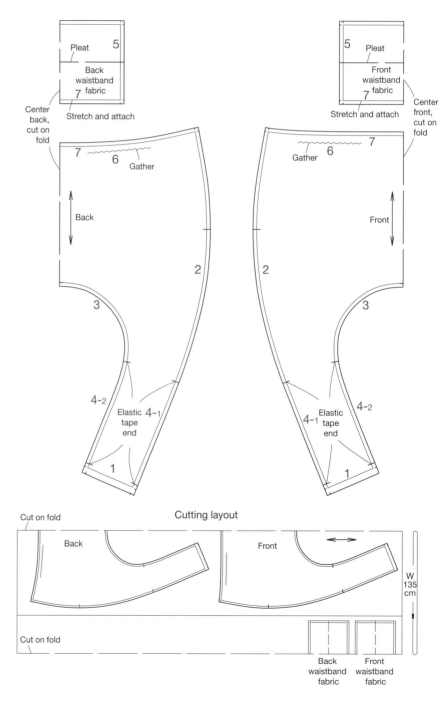

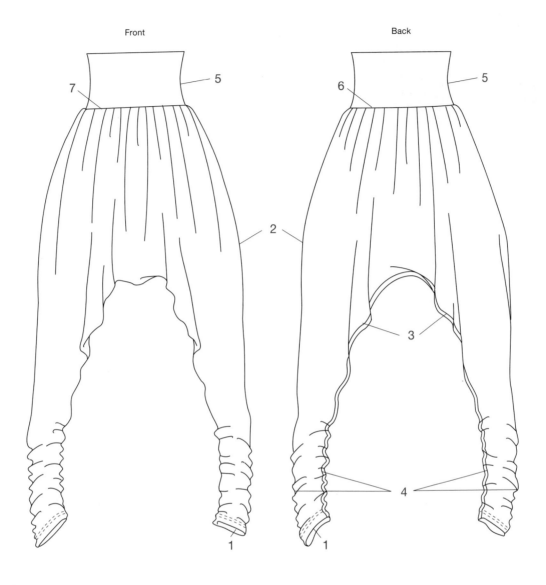

Front

Back

7

5

6

5

2

3

4

1

1

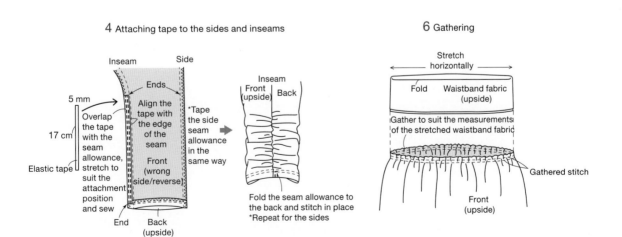

4 Attaching tape to the sides and inseams

Inseam   Side

Ends

5 mm

17 cm

Elastic tape

Overlap
the tape
with the
seam
allowance,
stretch to
suit the
attachment
position
and sew

Align the
tape with
the edge
of the
seam

Front
(wrong
side/reverse)

*Tape
the side
seam
allowance
in the
same way

End   Back
(upside)

Inseam
Front   Back
(upside)

Fold the seam allowance to
the back and stitch in place
*Repeat for the sides

6 Gathering

Stretch
horizontally

Fold   Waistband fabric
(upside)

Gather to suit the measurements
of the stretched waistband fabric

Gathered stitch

Front
(upside)

no.3 drop-waist gather drape dress

◆ **Required patterns (side A):**

front and back (align the bodice with the skirt).

◆ **Sewing instructions**

1 Finish the neckline and armholes with a threefold edge-stitched seam. The armholes are connected to the back design lines, so make a slit in the sleeve ends, and finish the armholes only (see figures 1 and 2).
2 Gather the sleeves and sew onto the bodice (see figures 1 and 2).
3 Gather the skirt and sew onto the upper bodice (see figure 3).
4 Sew the center back and attach an invisible zipper. See p. 39 for instructions on attaching a zipper.
5 Fold up the hem, and stitch.

◆ **Widths and lengths used**

Material: wool jersey (plain knit)
= W 150 cm
(S) 1 m 10 cm
(M) 1 m 20 cm
(L) 1 m 30 cm
(XL) 1 m 40 cm
56 cm invisible zipper

Cutting layout

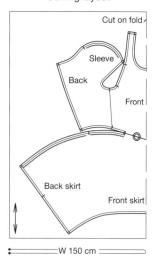

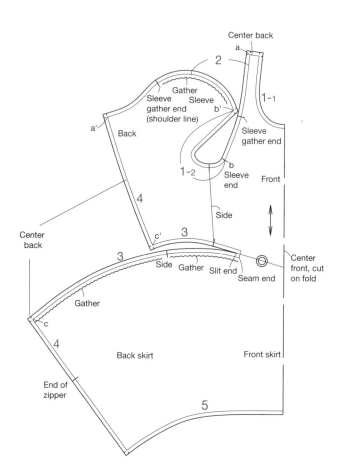

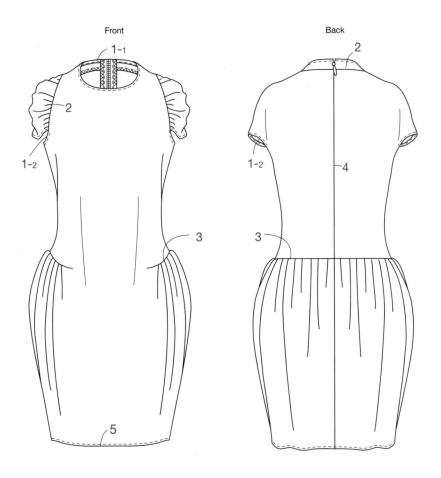

Front

Back

1-1

2

1-2

2

1-2

4

3

3

3

5

1, 2 Finishing the neckline and armholes and attaching the sleeves

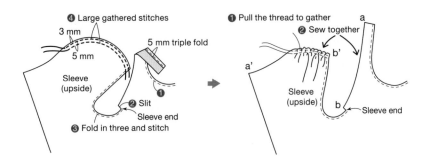

❹ Large gathered stitches

3 mm

5 mm

5 mm triple fold

Sleeve
(upside)

❷ Slit

Sleeve end

❸ Fold in three and stitch

❶ Pull the thread to gather

a

❷ Sew together

b'

a'

Sleeve
(upside)

b

Sleeve end

3 Sewing up the skirt and bodice

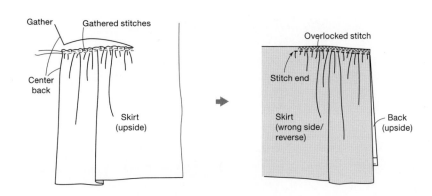

Gather

Gathered stitches

Center
back

Skirt
(upside)

Overlocked stitch

Stitch end

Skirt
(wrong side/
reverse)

Back
(upside)

no.4 panel drape dress
see page 30 for instructions

no.5 v-neck drape drape dress
see page 36 for instructions

no.4 panel drape dress

◆ **Required patterns (side B):**

front (align the panel, neckline, hem, and hem sides),
back (align the panel, neckline, and hem),
panel loop, front facing, back facing, front lining, back lining.

◆ **Sewing instructions**

* Attach fusible interlining to the front and back facing.

1 Finish the perimeter of the front and back panels with a threefold edge-stitched seam (see figure 1 on p. 32).

2 Fold the tucks on the bodice back neckline (see figure 2 on p. 32).

3 Fold the tucks on the bodice front neckline (see figure 3 on p. 32).

4 Sew up the shoulders on the bodice and facing (see figure 4 on p. 33).

5 Make a loop for the panel and tack onto the left shoulder (see figure 5 on p. 33).

6 Edge-stitch (lap-seam) the neckline with the facing (see figure 6 on p. 33).

7 Edge-stitch (lap-seam) the armholes with the facing.

8 Sew the sides of the bodice and facing so they are adjoining, adding a lapped seam to the seam allowance on the armholes.

9 Arrange the tucks on the bodice front neckline and sew in place behind the panel loop (see figure 9 on p. 33).

10 Sew the sides of the lining.

11 Fold the tucks in the bodice neck (on the upside) and sew onto the hem of the lining.

12 Fold the upper edge seam allowance on the bodice lining, and blindstitch to the facing.

◆ **Widths and lengths used**

Material: matte jersey (plain knit)
= W 150 cm
(S) 3 m 10 cm, (M) 3 m 10 cm
(L) 3 m 10 cm, (XL) 3 m 10 cm
Reverse (for knits)
= W 90 cm
(S) 1 m 50 cm, (M) 1 m 60 cm
(L) 1 m 70 cm, (XL) 1 m 80 cm
Fusible interlining (for knits)
= W 90 cm x L 30 cm

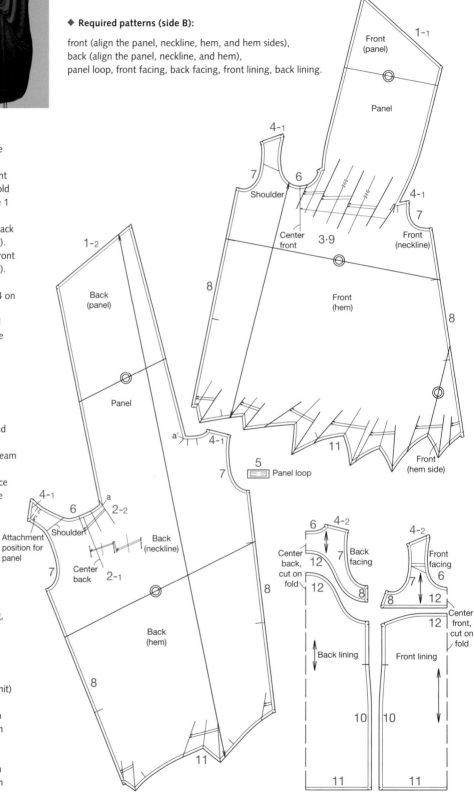

Front   Left side (for back see p. 32)

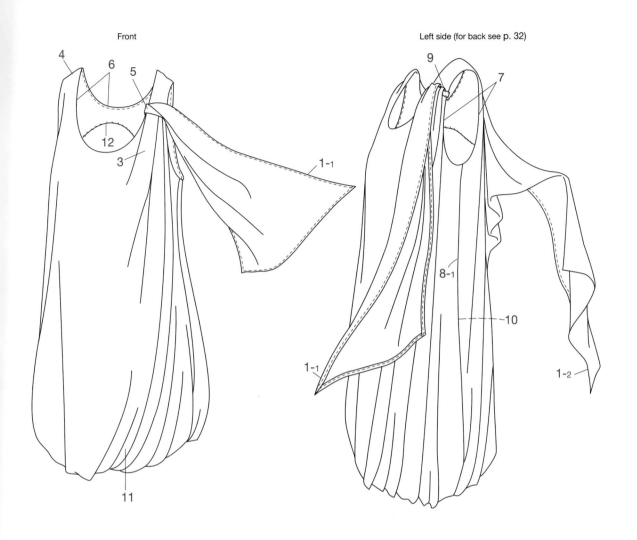

4
6 5
12
3
1-1
11

9
7
8-1
10
1-1
1-2

Cutting layout

Front
Panel
Panel
Back
Panel loop

Front facing
Back facing

W
150
cm

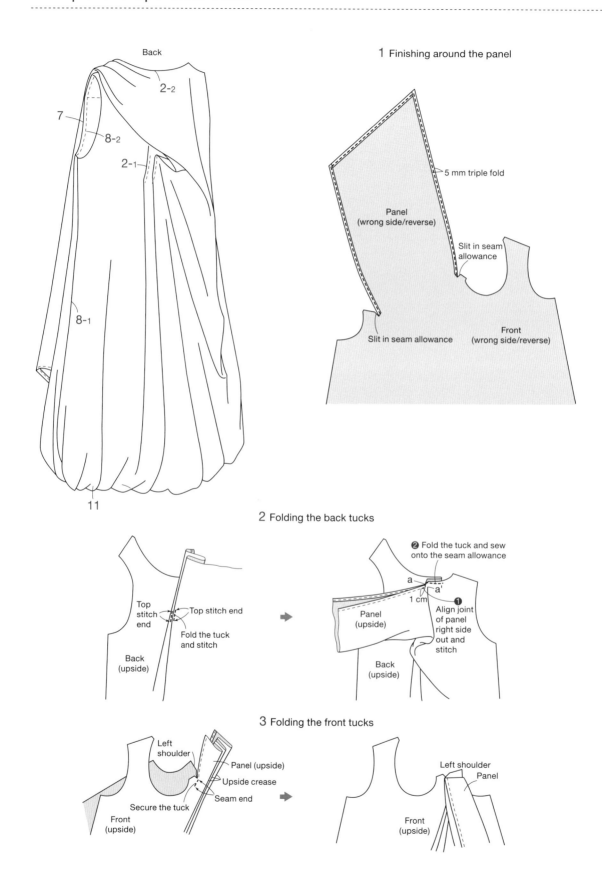

Back

2-2

7

8-2

2-1

8-1

11

1 Finishing around the panel

5 mm triple fold

Panel
(wrong side/reverse)

Slit in seam
allowance

Slit in seam allowance

Front
(wrong side/reverse)

2 Folding the back tucks

Top
stitch
end

Top stitch end

Fold the tuck
and stitch

Back
(upside)

❷ Fold the tuck and sew
onto the seam allowance

a

a'

1 cm

❶ Align joint
of panel
right side
out and
stitch

Panel
(upside)

Back
(upside)

3 Folding the front tucks

Left
shoulder

Panel (upside)

Upside crease

Seam end

Secure the tuck

Front
(upside)

Left shoulder

Panel

Front
(upside)

4 Sewing the shoulders

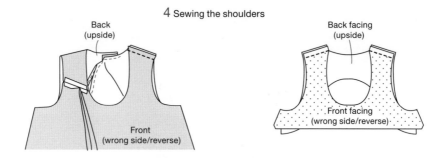

Back (upside)

Front (wrong side/reverse)

Back facing (upside)

Front facing (wrong side/reverse)

5 Attaching the loop for the panel

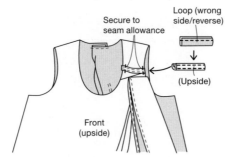

Secure to seam allowance

Loop (wrong side/reverse)

(Upside)

Front (upside)

6 Sewing the neckline

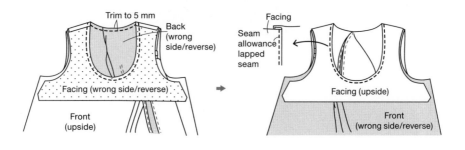

Trim to 5 mm

Back (wrong side/reverse)

Facing (wrong side/reverse)

Front (upside)

Facing

Seam allowance lapped seam

Facing (upside)

Front (wrong side/reverse)

9 Securing the front tucks

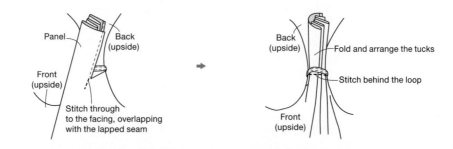

Panel

Front (upside)

Back (upside)

Stitch through to the facing, overlapping with the lapped seam

Back (upside)

Fold and arrange the tucks

Stitch behind the loop

Front (upside)

no.5 v-neck drape drape dress
see page 36 for instructions

no.5 v-neck drape drape dress

◆ **Required patterns (side B):**

back and back lining, front and front lining, back waist fabric and back waist fabric lining, front waist fabric and front waist fabric lining, front and back skirts (align the front and back).

◆ **Sewing instructions**

* Attach fusible interlining to the upside of the waist fabric.
1 Add gathers to the front.
2 Sew the darts in the front lining.
3 Sew together each of the shoulders on the upside and lining of the bodice.
4 Sew the necklines on the upside and lining of the bodice together (see figure 4 on p. 38).
5 Align the armholes on the upside and lining of the bodice, wrong side (reverse) out, and stitch with a margin of 3 to 4 cm from the sides before turning onto the upside.
6 Sew the sides on the upside and lining of the bodice together.
7 The armholes are still to be sewn. Stitch them wrong side (reverse) out (see figure 7 on p. 38).
8 Overlap the left and right of the bodice front by aligning the center fronts, and tack in place (see figure 8 on p. 38).
9 Sew the sides of the upside and lining of the waist fabric together.
10 Align the upside and lining of the waist fabric wrong side (reverse) out and sew, sandwiching the bodice at the top.
11 Fold the tucks in the front and back skirts and tack in place (see figure 11 on p. 38).
12 Sew up the center front of the skirt.
13 Sew down from the end of the zipper on the center back of the skirt.

14 Finish the hem with a threefold edge-stitched seam.
15 Sew together the upside waist fabric and skirt.
16 Stitch the bottom of the waist fabric lining in place with a topstitched seam.
17 Attach an invisible zipper to the center back (see figure 17 on p. 39).

◆ **Widths and lengths used**

Upside material: matte jersey (plain knit)
= W 160 cm
(S, M) 2 m
(L, XL) 2 m 10 cm
Fusible interlining
W 90 cm x L 20 cm
56 cm invisible zipper

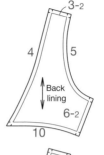
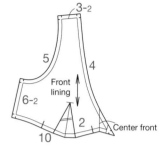
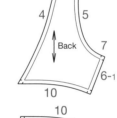
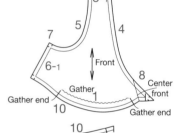
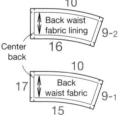
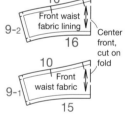
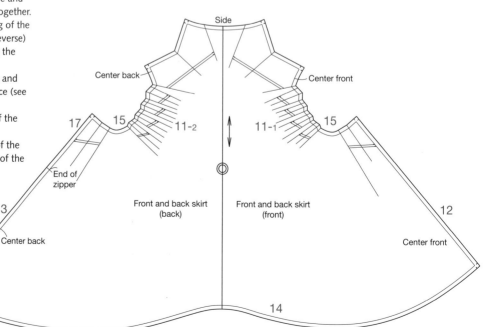

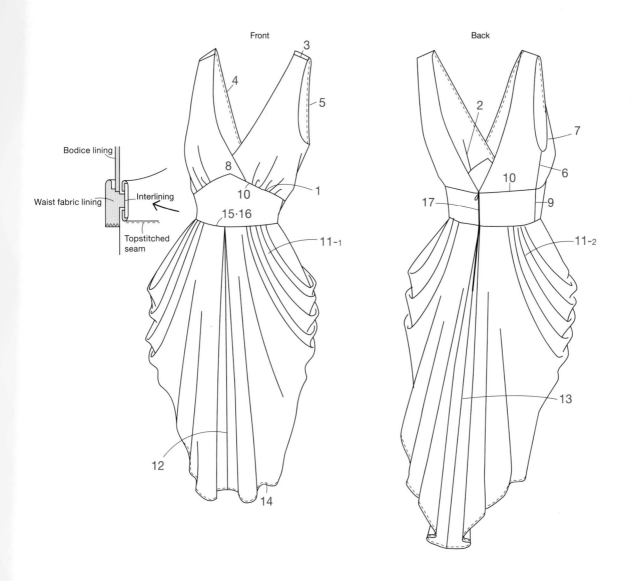

Front

Back

Bodice lining

Waist fabric lining

Interlining

Topstitched seam

3
4
5
8
10
1
15·16
11-1
12
14

2
7
6
10
9
17
11-2
13

Cutting layout

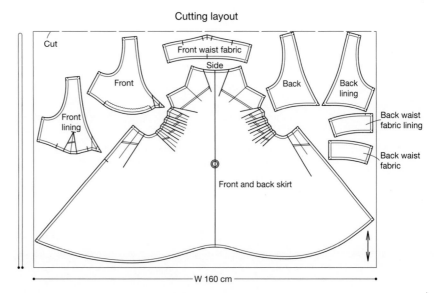

Cut

Front waist fabric

Side

Front

Back

Back lining

Front lining

Back waist fabric lining

Back waist fabric

Front and back skirt

W 160 cm

4 Sewing the neckline

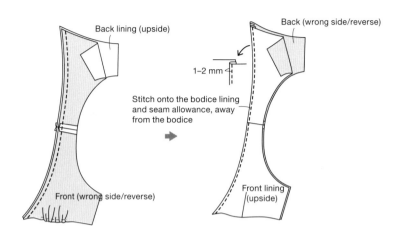

Back lining (upside)

Back (wrong side/reverse)

1–2 mm

Stitch onto the bodice lining and seam allowance, away from the bodice

Front lining (upside)

Front (wrong side/reverse)

7 Finishing the neckline

As far as you can stitch

1–2 mm

Front lining (upside)

❷ Stitch onto the bodice lining and seam allowance

Side

❶ Stitch the unsewn armhole right side out

Back (upside)

8 Aligning the center front

Back lining (upside)

Front (upside)

Align the center fronts, overlapping left and right, and stitch onto the seam allowance

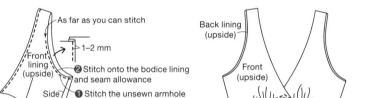

11 Folding the tucks

*The arrows show the direction in which the tucks are folded down

Fold the tucks and stitch to the seam allowance

Center back

Center front

Side

Skirt (upside)

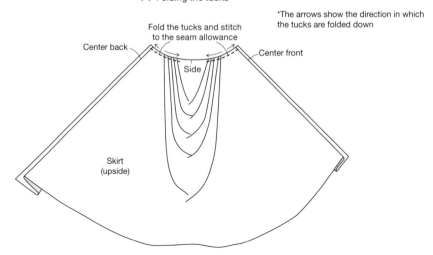

17 Attaching an invisible zipper

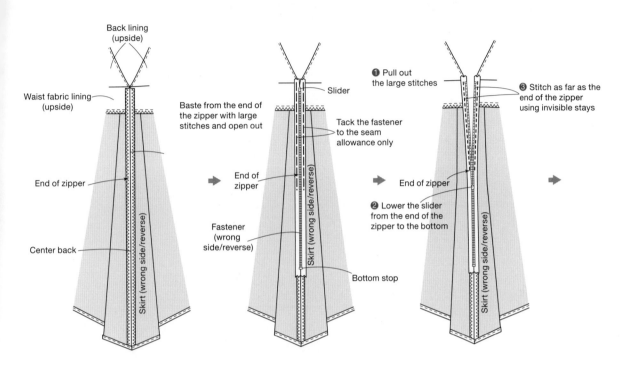

Back lining (upside)

Waist fabric lining (upside)

End of zipper

Center back

Skirt (wrong side/reverse)

Baste from the end of the zipper with large stitches and open out

End of zipper

Fastener (wrong side/reverse)

Skirt (wrong side/reverse)

Slider

Tack the fastener to the seam allowance only

Bottom stop

❶ Pull out the large stitches

End of zipper

❷ Lower the slider from the end of the zipper to the bottom

❸ Stitch as far as the end of the zipper using invisible stays

Skirt (wrong side/reverse)

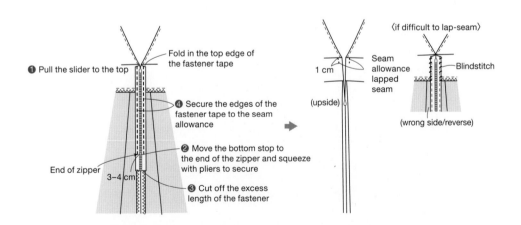

❶ Pull the slider to the top

Fold in the top edge of the fastener tape

❹ Secure the edges of the fastener tape to the seam allowance

❷ Move the bottom stop to the end of the zipper and squeeze with pliers to secure

❸ Cut off the excess length of the fastener

End of zipper

3–4 cm

1 cm

(upside)

Seam allowance lapped seam

⟨if difficult to lap-seam⟩

Blindstitch

(wrong side/reverse)

no.6 low-back gather drape dress
see page 42 for instructions

no.6 low-back gather drape dress

◆ **Required patterns (side B):**

top right, top left, bottom right, bottom left (align the top, bottom, left, and right),
back neckline hemming fabric, front neckline hemming fabric, armhole hemming fabric.

◆ **Sewing instructions**

1 Sew the shoulders together.
2 Sew the center back together.
3 Hem the armholes.
4 Gather the back neckline
   (see figure 4). Fold the tuck and
   then tack in place.
5 Hem the neckline.
6 Fold up the hem and stitch.

◆ **Widths and lengths used**

Material: rayon doubleknit
   (double rib)
= W 160 cm
(S, M) 1 m 50 cm
(L, XL) 1 m 60 cm

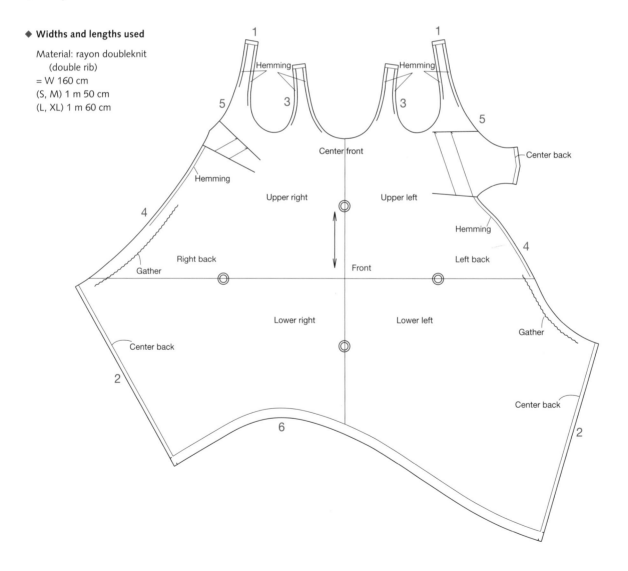

Front

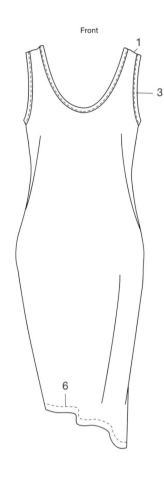

1

3

6

Back

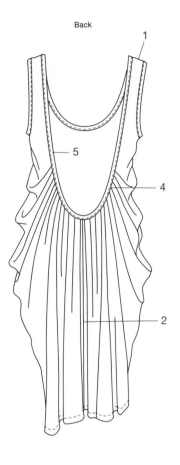

1

5

4

2

Cutting layout

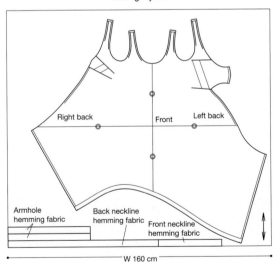

Right back

Front

Left back

Armhole
hemming fabric

Back neckline
hemming fabric

Front neckline
hemming fabric

W 160 cm

4 Gathering

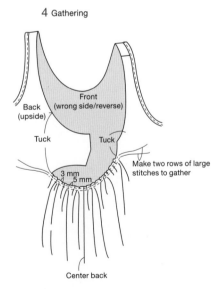

Back
(upside)

Front
(wrong side/reverse)

Tuck

Tuck

3 mm

5 mm

Make two rows of large
stitches to gather

Center back

no.7 gather drape blouse
see page 46 for instructions

no.7 gather drape blouse

◆ **Required patterns (side C):**

front, back (align the front and back).

◆ **Sewing instructions**

1 Finish the front and back hems, cuffs, and neckline with a threefold edge-stitched seam.
2 French-seam the center front together. See p. 55 for instructions on french-seaming.
3 Make the front gather, then fold the center tucks and stitch in place (see figure 3).
4 French-seam the center back together.
5 French-seam the sides together from cuff to hem.

◆ **Widths and lengths used**

Material: polyester chiffon
= W 112 cm
(S, M) 3 m 20 cm
(L, XL) 3 m 40 cm

Cutting layout

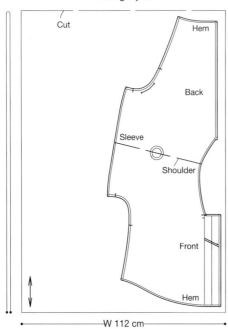

W 112 cm

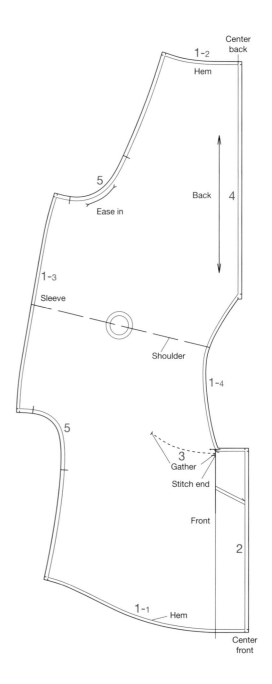

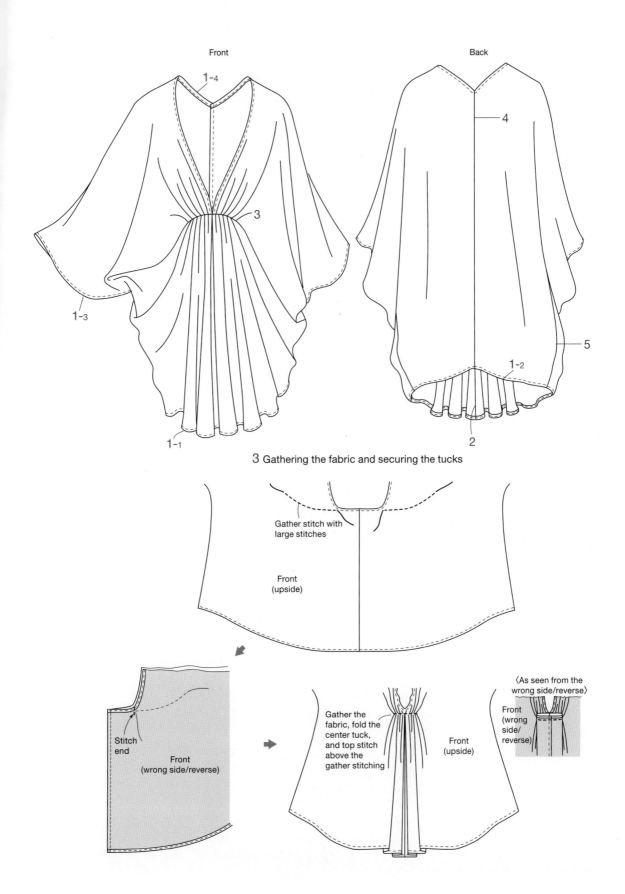

Front

1-4

3

1-3

1-1

Back

4

5

1-2

2

3 Gathering the fabric and securing the tucks

Gather stitch with
large stitches

Front
(upside)

Stitch
end

Front
(wrong side/reverse)

Gather the
fabric, fold the
center tuck,
and top stitch
above the
gather stitching

Front
(upside)

⟨As seen from the
wrong side/reverse⟩

Front
(wrong
side/
reverse)

no.8 drape drape all-in-one
see page 50 for instructions

no.8 drape drape all-in-one

◆ **Required patterns (side C):**

front and back (align the front and back), neckline.

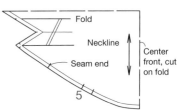

◆ **Sewing instructions**

1 Fold the seam allowances on the back neckline and front and back armholes to their respective seam ends and stitch them in place.
2 Sew the inseams together.
3 Fold up the hem, and stitch.
4 Sew the front and back seams for the leg openings together so that they are adjoining.
5 Fold the tucks at the center front and neckline. Attach the neckline to the front (see figure 5).
6 Stitch the back tucks in place, wrong side (reverse) out, and fix at the center back (see figure 6).
7 Sew the shoulders together.
8 Divide the shoulder area above the seam ends on the armholes and neckline into front and back sections and sew them together into a roll (see figure 8).

◆ **Widths and lengths used**

Material: silk jersey (plain knit)
= W 150 cm
(S, M) 2 m 40 cm
(L, XL) 2 m 60 cm

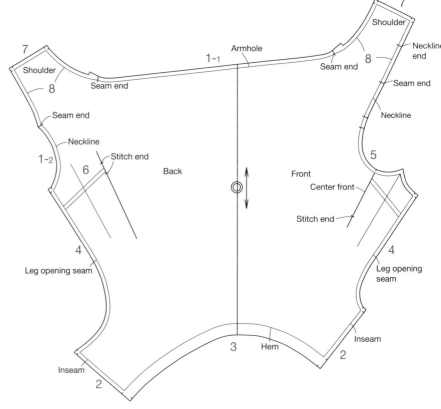

Cutting layout

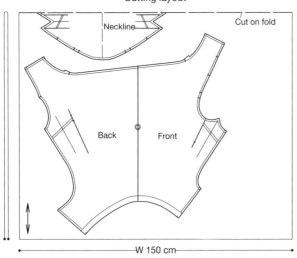

6 Sewing the back tuck

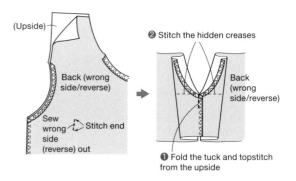

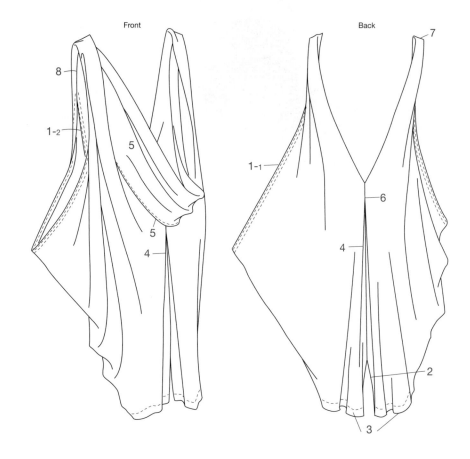

Front

Back

8

1-2

5

5

4

7

1-1

6

4

2

3

5 Attaching the neckline

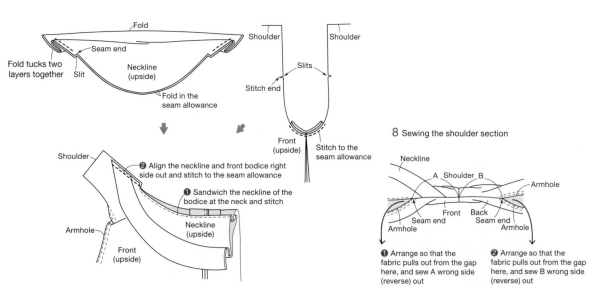

Fold

Seam end

Fold tucks two
layers together

Slit

Neckline
(upside)

Fold in the
seam allowance

Shoulder

Shoulder

Slits

Stitch end

Front
(upside)

Stitch to the
seam allowance

Shoulder

❷ Align the neckline and front bodice right
side out and stitch to the seam allowance

❶ Sandwich the neckline of the
bodice at the neck and stitch

Armhole

Front
(upside)

Neckline
(upside)

8 Sewing the shoulder section

Neckline

A Shoulder B

Armhole

Front   Back

Armhole

Seam end

Seam end

Armhole

❶ Arrange so that the
fabric pulls out from the gap
here, and sew A wrong side
(reverse) out

❷ Arrange so that the
fabric pulls out from the gap
here, and sew B wrong side
(reverse) out

no.9 loose drape blouse
see page 54 for instructions

no.9 loose drape blouse

◆ **Required patterns (side C):**

front, back (align the front and back), neckline fabric, center back fabric (align the front and back), cuffs.

◆ **Sewing instructions**

1 Finish the seam allowance in the areas of the bodice where the lace will be applied with a threefold edge-stitched seam.
2 Attach the lace to the bodice.
3 Sew the hem from the seam end, overlapping with the center back of the lace.
4 French-seam the front and back side seams to the sleeve seams (see figure 4).
5 Finish the hem with a threefold edge-stitched seam.
6 For the cuffs, connect two pieces of overlapping, 9 cm-wide lace and french-seam the side seams together.
7 Gather the cuffs and attach them.
8 Apply elastic tape to the inside of the fabric where the cuffs will be attached. Ensuring that the elastic tape is 3 cm shorter than the measurement of the cuffs, stretch and sew in place.

◆ **Widths and lengths used**

Materials: cotton and cupra rayon chiffon
= W 145 cm x L 2 m 60 cm
Lace
= W 9 cm x L 3 m 80 cm
1 cm-wide elastic tape, to fit

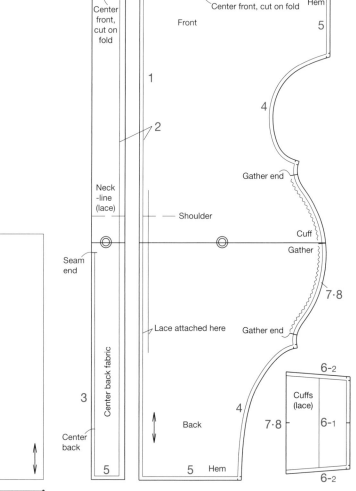

Cutting layout

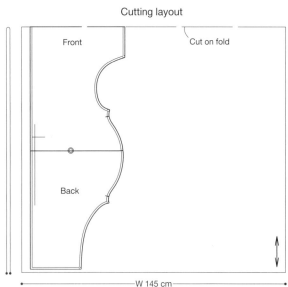

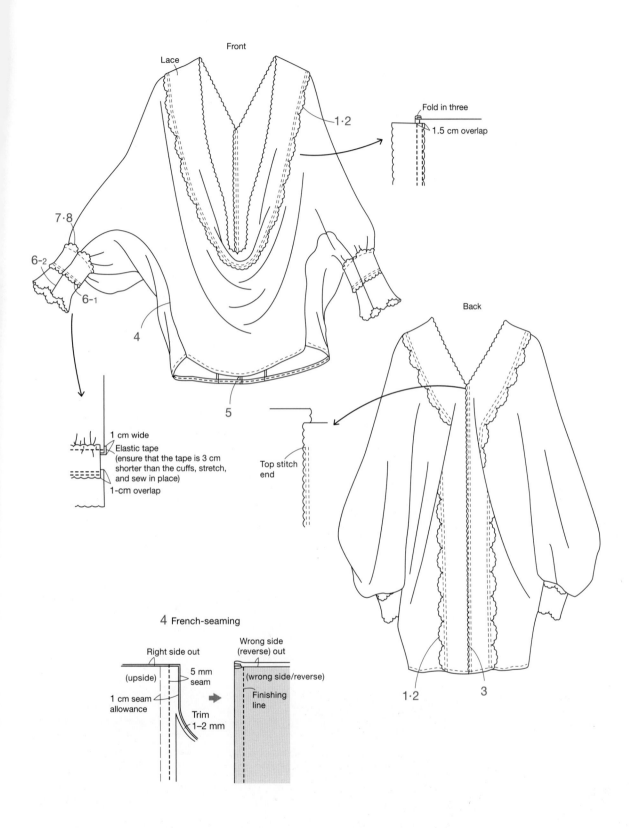

Front

Lace

1·2

Fold in three

1.5 cm overlap

7·8

6-2

6-1

4

5

1 cm wide

Elastic tape
(ensure that the tape is 3 cm
shorter than the cuffs, stretch,
and sew in place)

1-cm overlap

Top stitch
end

Back

1·2

3

4 French-seaming

Right side out

(upside)

5 mm
seam

1 cm seam
allowance

Trim
1–2 mm

Wrong side
(reverse) out

(wrong side/reverse)

Finishing
line

no.10 tuck drape dress
see page 58 for instructions

no.10 tuck drape dress

◆ **Required patterns (side C):**

front, back (align the front and back), back yoke, front yoke.

◆ **Sewing instructions**

* Attach fusible interlining to the yoke lining.
1 Sew up each of the shoulders on the upside and lining of the yokes.
2 Edge-stitch the neckline and armholes on the upside and lining of the yokes.
3 Sew the center back of the upside and lining of the yokes together.
4 Sew the center back together.
5 Sew the center back to the seam end of the tuck and then fold the tucks (in an inverted pleat).
6 Fold the front tucks, turn up the facing, and tack in place (see figure 6).
7 Attach the yokes to the bodice.
8 Fold up the hem, and stitch.

◆ **Widths and lengths used**

Material: matte jersey (plain knit)
= W 110 cm
(S) 2 m 10 cm, (M) 2 m 20 cm
(L) 2 m 30 cm, (XL) 2 m 40 cm
Other fabric for yokes: silk satin
= W 90 cm x L 50 cm
Fusible interlining
= W 90 cm x L 30 cm

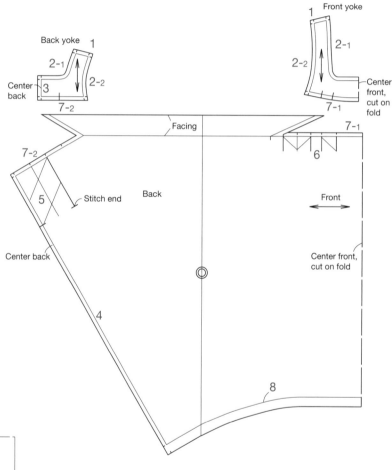

Cutting layout for upside fabric

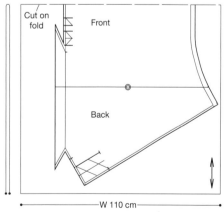

Cutting layout for
separate yoke fabric

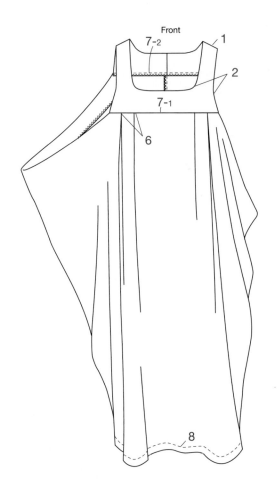

Front

7-2

1

2

7-1

6

8

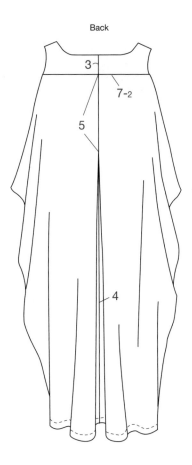

Back

3

7-2

5

4

6 Folding the front tucks

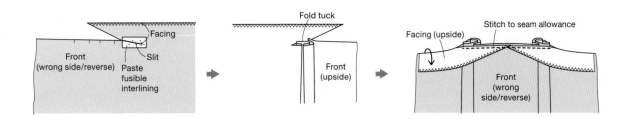

Facing

Front
(wrong side/reverse)

Slit

Paste
fusible
interlining

Fold tuck

Front
(upside)

Facing (upside)

Stitch to seam allowance

Front
(wrong
side/reverse)

no.11 loose flare drape dress
see page 62 for instructions

no.12 drawstring-
detail drape top
see page 66 for instructions

no.11 loose flare drape dress

◆ **Required patterns (side C):**

front (align the right and left), back, front panel (align the right and left), front left armhole fabric, front facing, back facing, back lining, front lining.

◆ **Sewing instructions**

1 Finish the front edge of the front panel, the hem, and the armholes with a threefold edge-stitched seam (see figure 1 on p. 64).

2 Sew the right sides of the facing and lining.

3 Sew together the facing and lining. Sew the back lining sandwiched between the two back facings (see figure 3 on p. 64).

4 Sew together the right side of the dress.

5 Align the bodice from step 4 with the bodice lining from step 3, wrong side (reverse) out and, interposing the panel at the center back, sew as follows: back top edge—right armhole—center back—neckline. Turn the garment to the upside, passing the elastic tape through the back facing (see figure 5 on p. 64).

6 Tack the left side of the panel to the left side of the front bodice (see figure 6 on p. 65).

7 Edge-stitch the front left armhole with the armhole fabric (see figure 7 on p. 65).

8 Sew the left side of the dress and attach an invisible zipper. See p. 39 for instructions on attaching a zipper.

9 Sew the left side of the lining, stitch the left armhole fabric in place, then fold and blind-stitch the seam allowance of the opening (see figure 6 on p. 65).

10 Finish the hems on the upside and wrong side (reverse) of the fabric with threefold edge-stitched seams.

◆ **Widths and lengths used**

Material: georgette
= W 112cm
(S) 2 m 20 cm
(M) 2 m 30 cm
(L) 2 m 40 cm
(XL) 2 m 50 cm
Lining
W 110 cm
(S/M) 1 m 30 cm
(M/L) 1 m 50 cm
5 cm-wide elastic tape, to fit
1 x 56 cm invisible zipper

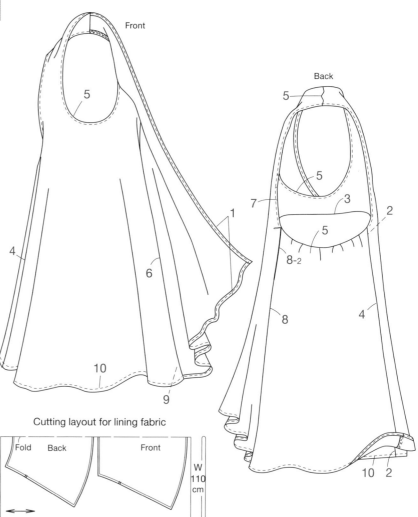

Cutting layout for lining fabric

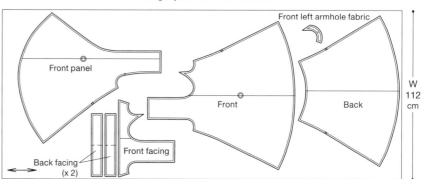

Cutting layout for dress material

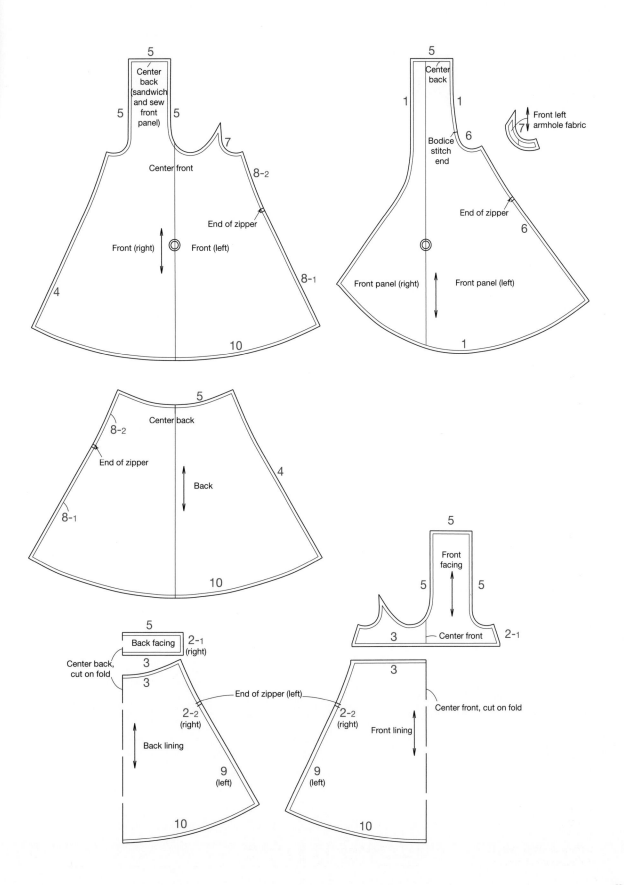

5

Center back (sandwich and sew front panel)

5   5

Center front

7

8-2

End of zipper

Front (right)   Front (left)

4

8-1

10

5

Center back

Bodice stitch end

1   1

6

Front left armhole fabric

7

End of zipper

6

Front panel (right)   Front panel (left)

1

5

Center back

8-2

End of zipper

Back

4

8-1

10

5

Front facing

5   5

3   Center front   2-1

5

Back facing   2-1 (right)

Center back, cut on fold

3

3

2-2 (right)

End of zipper (left)

2-2 (right)

3

Center front, cut on fold

Back lining

Front lining

9 (left)   9 (left)

10   10

63

no.11 loose flare drape dress continued

1 Finishing around the panel

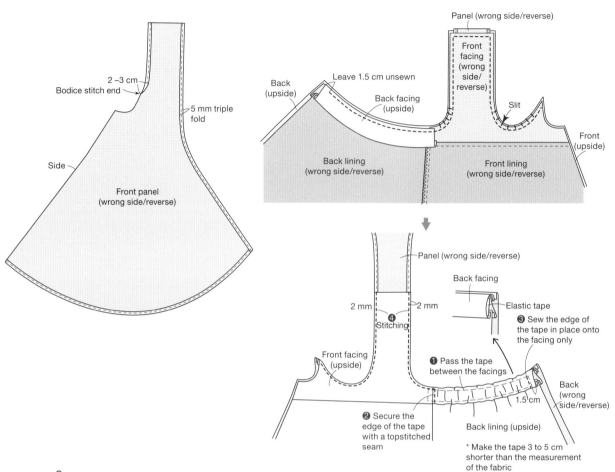

1 (Finishing around the panel diagram labels):
- 2 –3 cm
- Bodice stitch end
- 5 mm triple fold
- Side
- Front panel (wrong side/reverse)

5 Sewing the upside and lining of the bodice

- Panel (wrong side/reverse)
- Front facing (wrong side/reverse)
- Leave 1.5 cm unsewn
- Back (upside)
- Back facing (upside)
- Slit
- Front (upside)
- Back lining (wrong side/reverse)
- Front lining (wrong side/reverse)

- Panel (wrong side/reverse)
- Back facing
- Elastic tape
- 2 mm   2 mm
- ❹ Stitching
- ❸ Sew the edge of the tape in place onto the facing only
- Front facing (upside)
- ❶ Pass the tape between the facings
- Back (wrong side/reverse)
- 1.5 cm
- ❷ Secure the edge of the tape with a topstitched seam
- Back lining (upside)
- * Make the tape 3 to 5 cm shorter than the measurement of the fabric

3 Sewing together the facings and lining

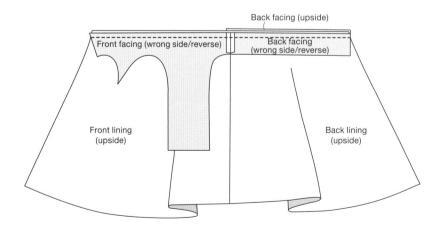

- Back facing (upside)
- Front facing (wrong side/reverse)
- Back facing (wrong side/reverse)
- Front lining (upside)
- Back lining (upside)

6 Tacking the panel at the side

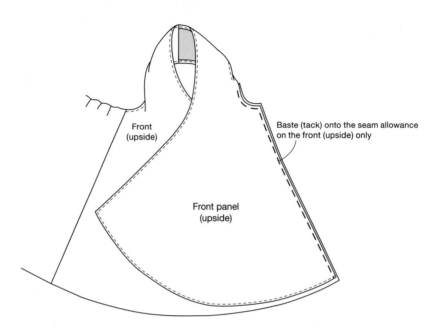

Front
(upside)

Baste (tack) onto the seam allowance
on the front (upside) only

Front panel
(upside)

7 Finishing the left armhole

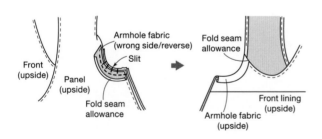

Front
(upside)

Panel
(upside)

Armhole fabric
(wrong side/reverse)

Slit

Fold seam
allowance

Fold seam
allowance

Front lining
(upside)

Armhole fabric
(upside)

9 Finishing the left side

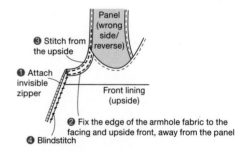

Panel
(wrong
side/
reverse)

❸ Stitch from
the upside

❶ Attach
invisible
zipper

Front lining
(upside)

❷ Fix the edge of the armhole fabric to the
facing and upside front, away from the panel

❹ Blindstitch

no.12 drawstring-detail drape top

◆ **Required patterns (side D):**

right back, left back, left front, right front (align the left back, left front, and right front).

◆ **Sewing instructions**

1 Sew the center back together.
2 Finish the back hem with a threefold edge-stitched seam.
3 Finish the neckline with a threefold edge-stitched seam. Fold the right side of the bodice front back from the hem so that the wrong side (reverse) of the fabric becomes the upside. At the right front neckline (3-2), triple-fold the seam allowance onto the upside of the fabric.
4 Finish the armholes with a threefold edge-stitched seam. At the armhole on the right side of the bodice front (4-2), triple-fold the seam allowance onto the upside of the fabric.

5 Fold the right side of the bodice front at the hem, fold the bodice back at the shoulders, and sew together the front and back sides at the left and right. On the right, this will mean sewing the back (upside) and front wrong side (reverse) in alignment.
6 Sew up the shoulders on the right side of the bodice front. When you do this, fold the seam allowance upwards with a flat-felled seam and then stitch to create the opening for the drawstrings.
7 Make the drawstrings, and pass them through the opening described in step 6.

◆ **Widths and lengths used**

Materials: silk and wool jersey (plain knit)
= W 140 cm
L 2 m 10 cm

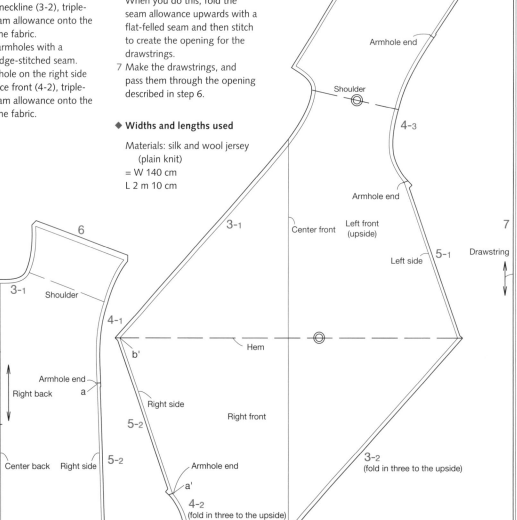

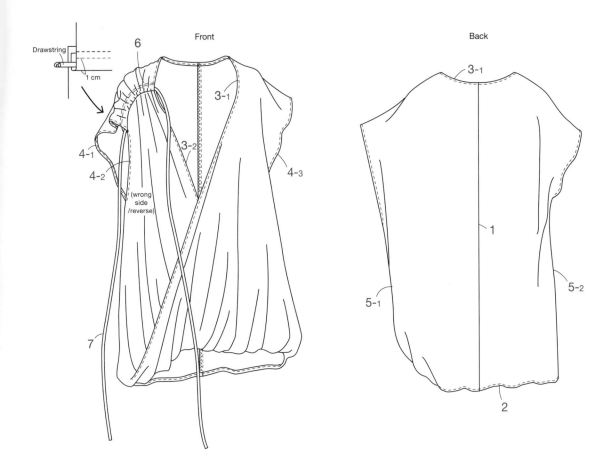

Drawstring
1 cm

6

Front

3-1

3-2

4-1

4-2

(wrong side /reverse)

4-3

7

Back

3-1

1

5-1

5-2

2

5 Sewing the sides

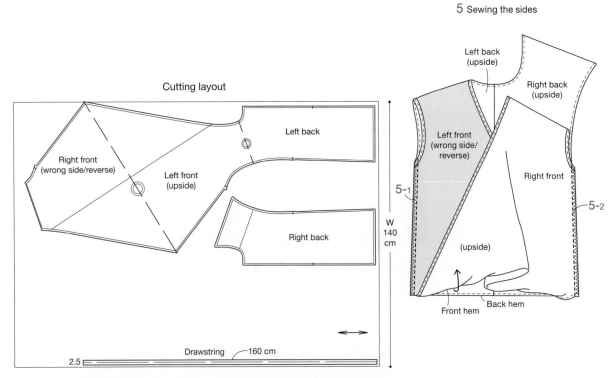

Cutting layout

Right front
(wrong side/reverse)

Left front
(upside)

Left back

Right back

W
140
cm

5-1

5-2

2.5

Drawstring — 160 cm

Left back
(upside)

Right back
(upside)

Left front
(wrong side/
reverse)

Right front

(upside)

Front hem

Back hem

no.13 loose drape tank-top
see page 70 for instructions

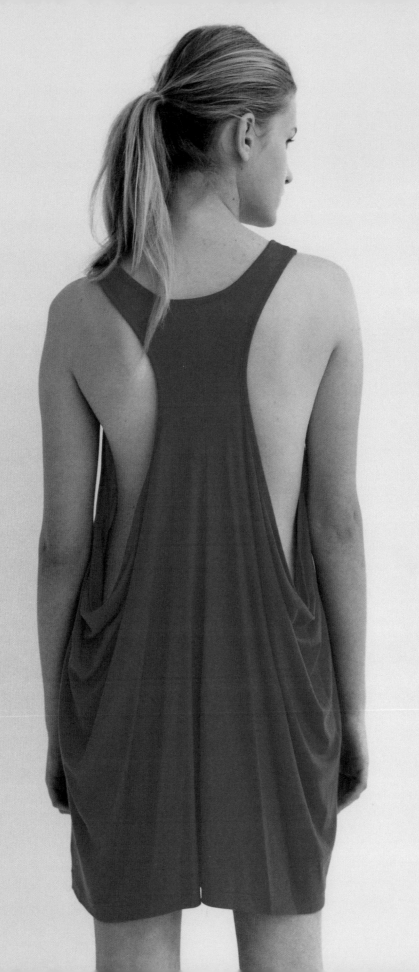

no.13 loose drape tank-top

◆ **Required patterns (side A):**

front, back (align the front and back).

◆ **Sewing instructions**

1 Sew the center back together.
2 Hem the neckline (see figure 2).
3 Hem the armholes.
4 Sew the shoulders together (see figure 4).
5 Fold up the hem, and stitch.

◆ **Widths and lengths used**

Material: rayon doubleknit
    (double rib)
= W 160 cm
(S, M) 1 m
(L, XL) 1 m 20 cm

Cutting layout

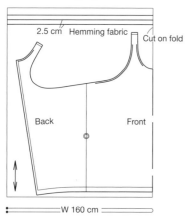

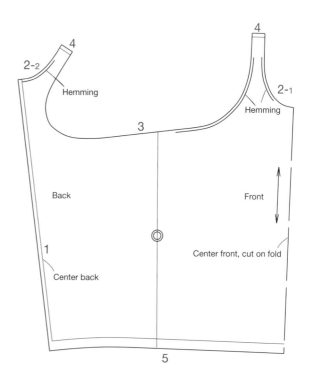

Front

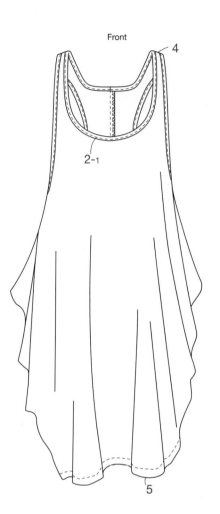

4

2-1

5

Back

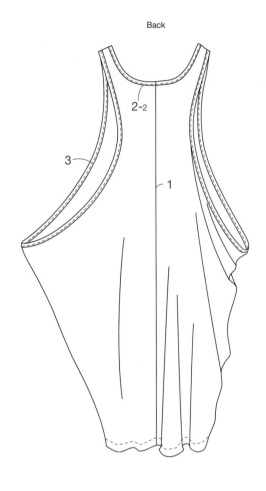

2-2

3

1

2 Hemming

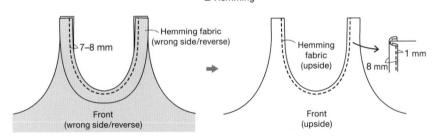

7–8 mm

Hemming fabric
(wrong side/reverse)

Front
(wrong side/reverse)

Hemming
fabric
(upside)

Front
(upside)

1 mm

8 mm

4 Sewing the shoulders

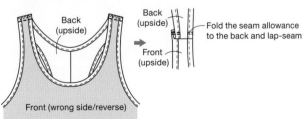

Back
(upside)

Front
(wrong side/reverse)

Back
(upside)

Front
(upside)

Fold the seam allowance
to the back and lap-seam

no.14 tuck drape lace tunic
see page 74 for instructions

no.15 loose drape frilled tunic
see page 76 for instructions

no.14 tuck drape lace tunic

◆ **Required patterns (side D):**

front, back (align the front and back), neckline hemming fabric and shoulder drawstring.

◆ **Sewing instructions**

1 Finish the left and right armholes with a threefold edge-stitched seam.

2 French-seam the center front and center back together. See p. 55 for instructions on french-seaming.

3 Stitch the center tucks on both front and back as far as the stitch end, and then fold the neckline tucks and tack in place (see figure 3).

4 Hem the neckline and make the shoulder drawstring.

5 Finish the hem with a threefold edge-stitched seam.

◆ **Widths and lengths used**

Material: lawn lace
= W 110 cm
(S, M) 2 m 50 cm
(L, XL) 2 m 70 cm

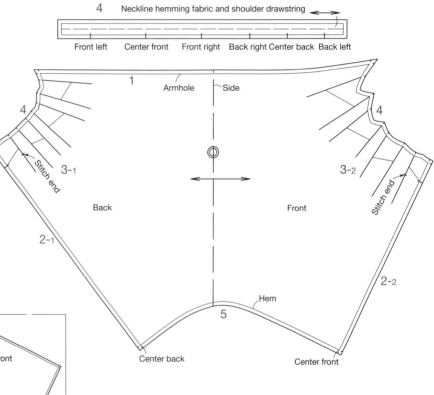

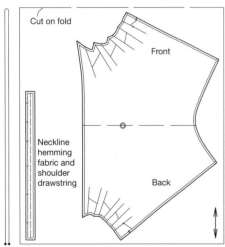

Front

4

1   3-2   1

2-2

5

Back

4

3-1

2-1

5

3 Folding the tucks

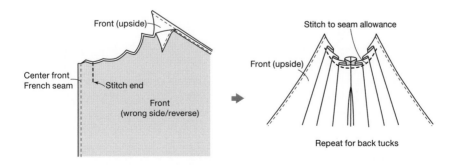

Front (upside)

Center front
French seam
Stitch end

Front
(wrong side/reverse)

Stitch to seam allowance

Front (upside)

Repeat for back tucks

no.15 loose drape frilled tunic

◆ **Required patterns (side D):**

front and back (align the front and back), back yoke, frill, hemming fabric.

◆ **Sewing instructions**

1 Sew the center back from the back yoke end to the hem.
2 Attach the back yoke to the center back.
3 Sew the sides from the armhole ends to the hem.
4 Attach lace A to the armholes.
5 Attach the hemming fabric (lace B).
6 Attach lace A to the neckline and the frill (lace B) to the front edge (see figure 6).
7 Add press studs to the inside of the front edge (see figure 7).

◆ **Widths and lengths used**

Material: cotton lace
= W 98 cm x L 1 m 90 cm
Lace A (neckline, armholes)
= W 2 cm x L 2 m 60 cm
Lace B (frill, hem fabric)
= W 20 cm x L 3 m 80 cm
Bias tape (double fold)
= W 1.2 cm x L 2 m

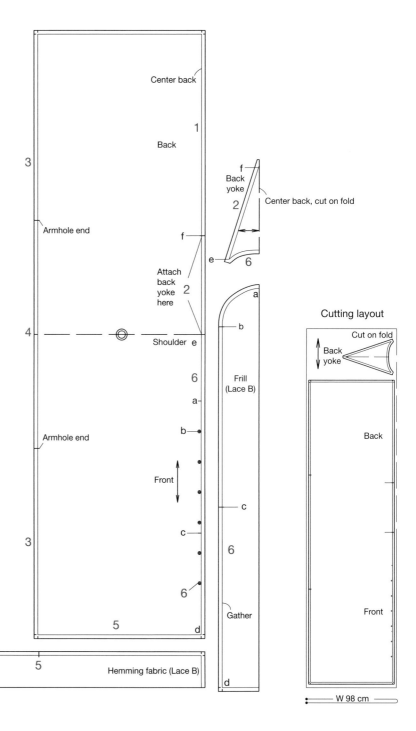

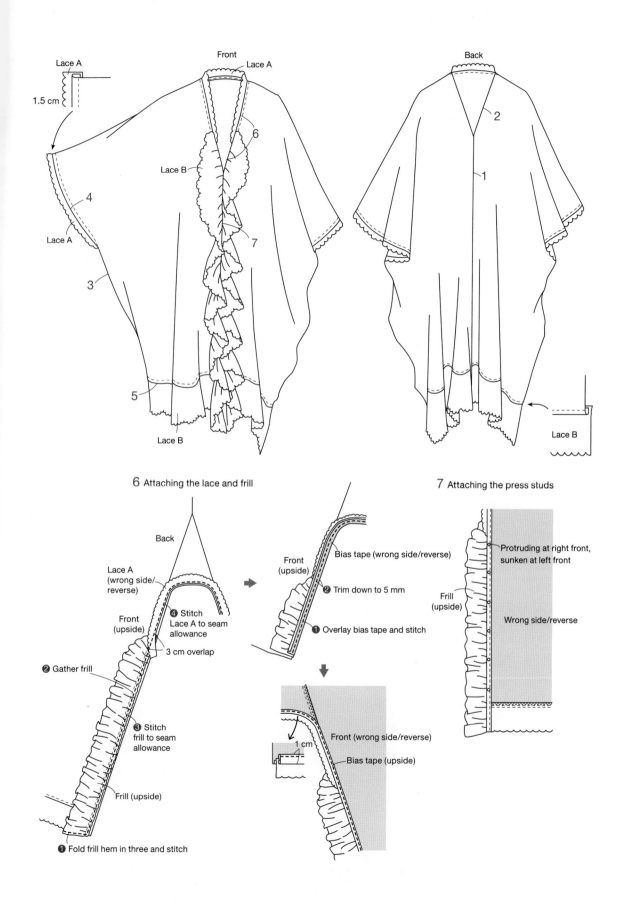

Lace A

1.5 cm

Front

Lace A

Lace B

6

7

4

Lace A

3

5

Lace B

Back

2

1

Lace B

6 Attaching the lace and frill

Back

Lace A
(wrong side/
reverse)

Front
(upside)

❹ Stitch
Lace A to seam
allowance

3 cm overlap

❷ Gather frill

❸ Stitch
frill to seam
allowance

Frill (upside)

❶ Fold frill hem in three and stitch

Front
(upside)

Bias tape (wrong side/reverse)

❷ Trim down to 5 mm

❶ Overlay bias tape and stitch

1 cm

Front (wrong side/reverse)

Bias tape (upside)

7 Attaching the press studs

Protruding at right front,
sunken at left front

Frill
(upside)

Wrong side/reverse

no.16 drape dress with
gathered sleeves
see page 80 for instructions

no.17 goddess drape dress
see page 84 for instructions

no.16 drape dress with gathered sleeves

◆ **Required patterns (side D):**

back, right front (align the collar and hem), left front, sleeves (align the sleeves, cuff backs, and cuff fronts), collar.

◆ **Sewing instructions**

1 Finish the hem on the bodice back and left and right sides of the bodice front and the seam allowance on the armholes with a threefold edge-stitched seam.

2 Fold the tucks on the right of the bodice front and tack in place (see figure 2 on p. 82). For further instructions on folding a tuck, see pp. 9–10.

3 Sew the shoulders together.

4 Attach the collar, fold the tucks at both ends (folding the two layers together) and tack in place (see figure 4 on p. 82).

5 Fold the sleeve tucks and tack in place (see figure 5 on p. 83).

6 Attach the sleeves.

7 Sew the sides and side seams together. When you do this, sew the front right edge of the collar into the left side seam (see figure 7 on p. 83).

8 Sew the front left edge of the collar to the seam allowance at the attachment position on the inside of the right side (see figure 8 on p. 83).

◆ **Widths and lengths used**

Material: silk jersey (plain knit)
= W 150 cm
(S) 2 m 30 cm
(M) 2 m 40 cm
(L) 2 m 50 cm
(XL) 2 m 60 cm

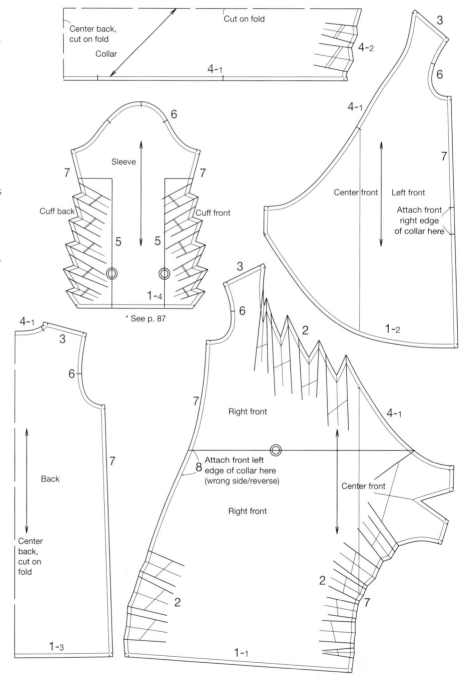

Front

Left side

6

4-1

7

5

1-4

2

4-2

1-2

1-1

3

6

7

7

1-4

1-3

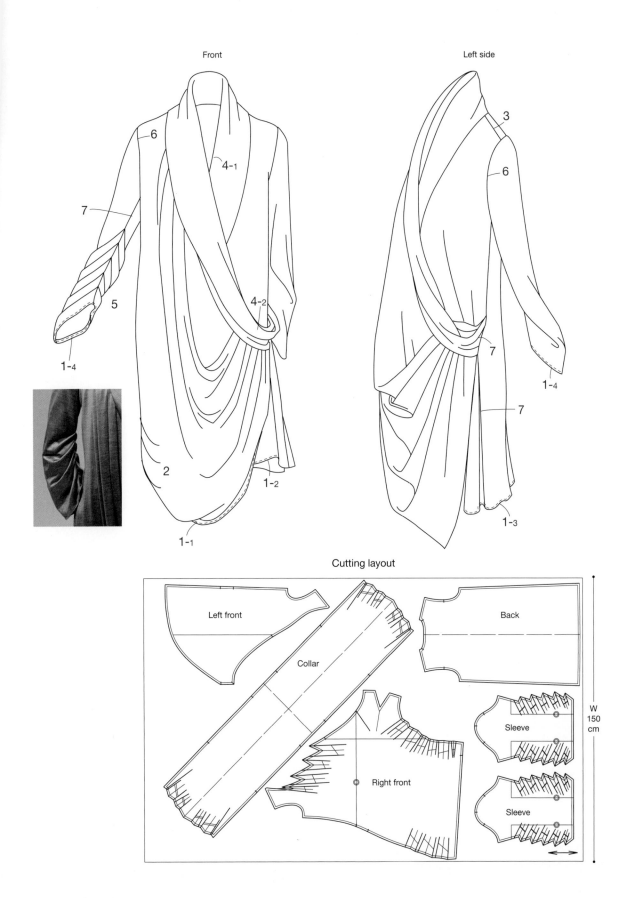

Cutting layout

Left front

Collar

Back

Sleeve

Right front

Sleeve

W
150
cm

2 Folding the right front tucks

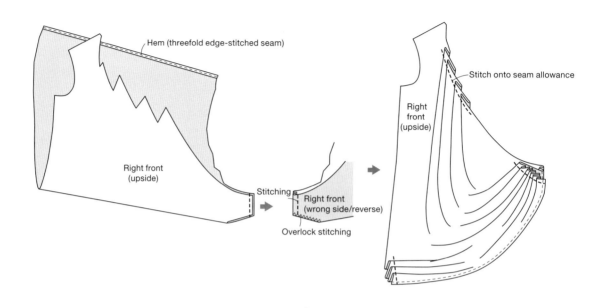

Hem (threefold edge-stitched seam)

Right front
(upside)

Stitching

Right front
(wrong side/reverse)

Overlock stitching

Right
front
(upside)

Stitch onto seam allowance

4 Attaching the collar

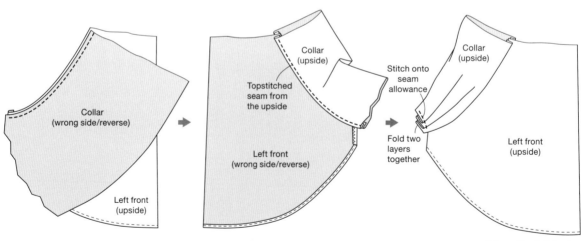

Collar
(wrong side/reverse)

Left front
(upside)

Collar
(upside)

Topstitched
seam from
the upside

Left front
(wrong side/reverse)

Stitch onto
seam
allowance

Fold two
layers
together

Collar
(upside)

Left front
(upside)

* Repeat for right front

5 Folding the sleeve tucks

Sleeve
(upside)

Stitch onto seam allowance

Threefold edge-stitched seam

8 Fixing the left front edge of the neck in place

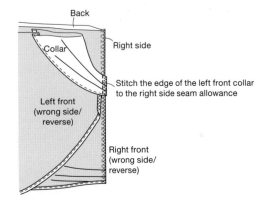

Back

Collar

Right side

Stitch the edge of the left front collar to the right side seam allowance

Left front
(wrong side/
reverse)

Right front
(wrong side/
reverse)

7 Sewing the sides and the side seams of the sleeves

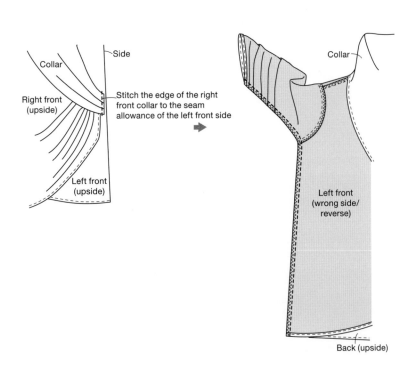

Side

Collar

Right front
(upside)

Stitch the edge of the right front collar to the seam allowance of the left front side

Left front
(upside)

Collar

Left front
(wrong side/
reverse)

Back (upside)

no.17 goddess drape dress

◆ **Required patterns (side D):**

front (align the neckline, front, and hem), back (align the neckline and hem).
*If you are using the S and M patterns, also align the right and left.

◆ **Sewing instructions**

1 Fold the front and back hems to the finishing line and stitch.
2 Fold the seam allowance on the front and back necklines and stitch (see figure 2 on p. 86).
3 Fold the tucks on the front and back bodices and tack in place (see figure 3 on p. 86).
4 Sew the shoulders together.
5 Finish the armholes with the hemming fabric (see figure 5 on p. 86).
6 Sew the sides together.

◆ **Widths and lengths used**

Material: matte jersey (plain knit)
= W 150 cm
(S, M) 3 m
(L, XL) 3 m 20 cm

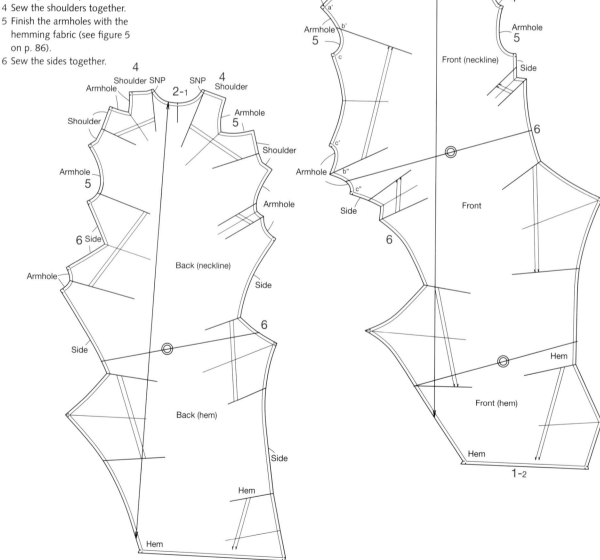

Front   Back

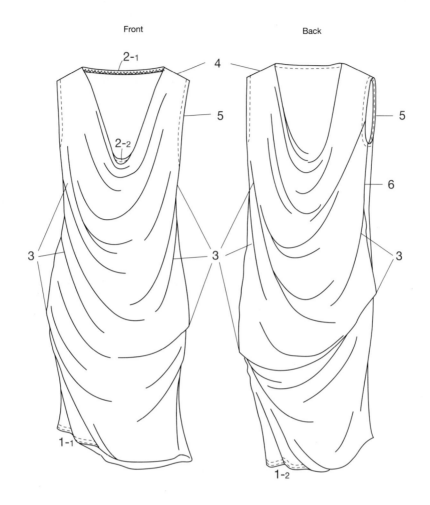

2-1
4
5
2-2
3   3   3   3
1-1
1-2

Cutting layout

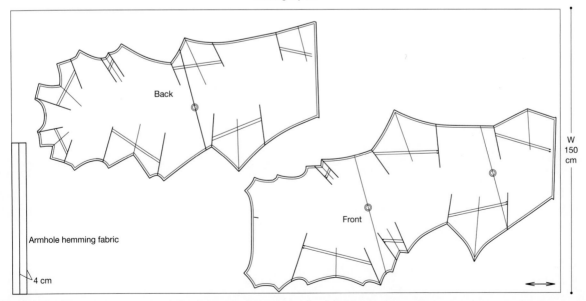

Back

Front

W
150
cm

Armhole hemming fabric

4 cm

2 Finishing the neckline

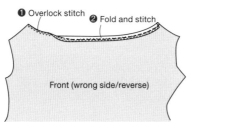

❶ Overlock stitch ❷ Fold and stitch

Front (wrong side/reverse)

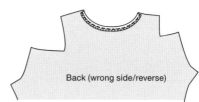

Back (wrong side/reverse)

3 Folding the tucks

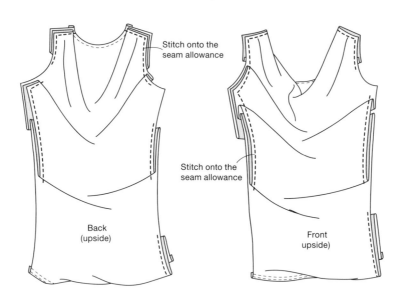

Stitch onto the seam allowance

Stitch onto the seam allowance

Back (upside)

Front upside)

5 Finishing the armholes

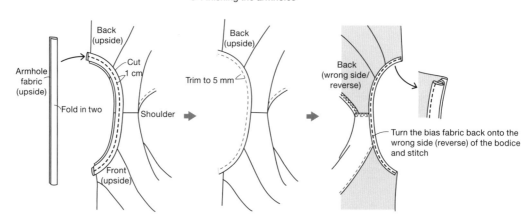

Armhole fabric (upside)

Back (upside)

Cut 1 cm

Fold in two

Shoulder

Front (upside)

Back (upside)

Trim to 5 mm

Back (wrong side/ reverse)

Turn the bias fabric back onto the wrong side (reverse) of the bodice and stitch

Before using the full-scale patterns

Please take a moment to review the different lines and markings shown on the full-scale patterns and how to use them.

◆ **Lines**

❶ Cutting line mark (seam allowance line)

❷ Finishing line (seam line)

❸ Grain

❹ Cut on the fold (fold line)

❺ Gather

❻ Ease in

◆ Direction of tuck folds   ◆ Alignment marking

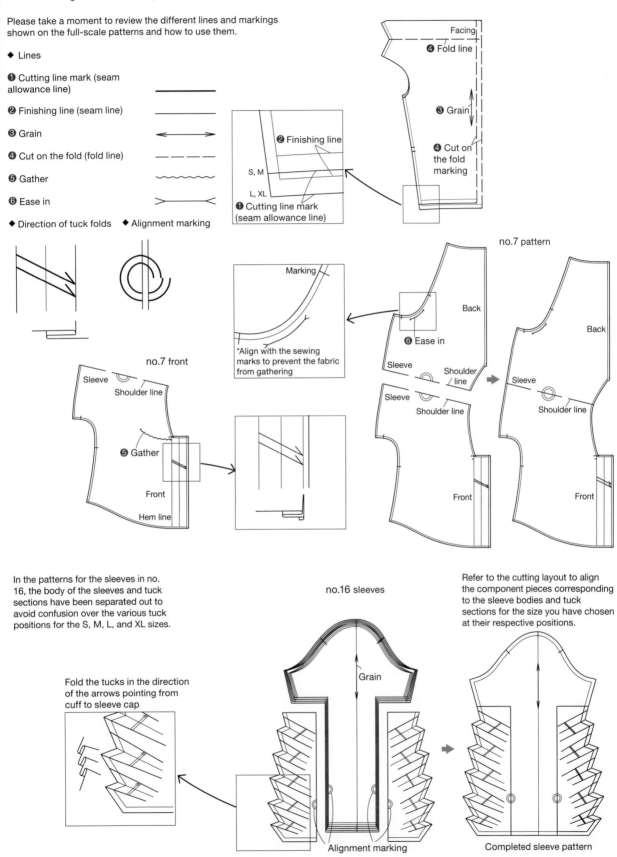

Facing
❹ Fold line
❸ Grain
❹ Cut on the fold marking

❷ Finishing line
S, M
L, XL
❶ Cutting line mark (seam allowance line)

Marking
*Align with the sewing marks to prevent the fabric from gathering

no.7 pattern

Back
❻ Ease in
Sleeve   Shoulder line
Sleeve
Shoulder line

Back
Sleeve
Shoulder line
Front

no.7 front
Sleeve
Shoulder line
❺ Gather
Front
Hem line

In the patterns for the sleeves in no. 16, the body of the sleeves and tuck sections have been separated out to avoid confusion over the various tuck positions for the S, M, L, and XL sizes.

no.16 sleeves

Refer to the cutting layout to align the component pieces corresponding to the sleeve bodies and tuck sections for the size you have chosen at their respective positions.

Fold the tucks in the direction of the arrows pointing from cuff to sleeve cap

Grain

Alignment marking

Completed sleeve pattern

Bibliography

The Essential Basics of Sewing Beautifully by Keiko Mizuno (BUNKA PUBLISHING BUREAU)

Sewing Lesson Note ABC by Naoko Domeki (BUNKA PUBLISHING BUREAU)

Fashion Dictionary (BUNKA PUBLISHING BUREAU)

Credits

Original Japanese edition

Publisher: Sunao Onuma, BUNKA PUBLISHING BUREAU
Editor: Nobuko Hirayama, BUNKA PUBLISHING BUREAU
Design and layout: Tomoko Nawada, L'Espace
Photography: Yasutomo Ebisu, Takeshi Fujimoto, BUNKA PUBLISHING BUREAU (pp. 33–84)
Hair and makeup: Hiromi Chinone
Model: Jessica. B, Ocean Moon
Pattern grading: Kazuhiro Ueno
Instructions: Keiko Mizuno (pp. 33–40), Naoko Domeki (pp. 41–86)
Tracing: Tomoko Fukushima

English edition

Translated from the Japanese by Andy Walker
Technical consultants: Chika Ito, Kevin Almond, Bo Breda
Design and typesetting: Mark Holt
Commissioning editor: Helen Rochester, Laurence King Publishing
Editor: Sarah Batten, Laurence King Publishing